The Flute

Keynote Books

By Bill Ballantine: THE VIOLIN

THE FLUTE

THE PIANO

Forthcoming Titles:

THE CLARINET

THE GUITAR

THE TRUMPET

DRUMS AND OTHER PERCUSSION INSTRUMENTS

THE CELLO

THE SAXOPHONE

THE TROMBONE

THE HORNS

THE OBOE

THE VIOLA

An eighteenth-century flutist.

A KEYNOTE BOOK

The Flute

An Introduction to the Instrument

by Bill Ballantine

Franklin Watts, Inc.
845 Third Avenue
New York, N.Y. 10022

We are grateful to the following for permission to reprint picture material:

The Dayton C. Miller Collection, Library of Congress (Frontispiece, pages 14, 21, 25, 27, 28, 29, 33, 40, 41, 46, 47, 48, 51, 52, 59, 64, 68, 76, 78, 80, 81, 82, 85, 95)

Prints and Photographs, Library of Congress (Pages 92, 96)

Smithsonian Institution (Pages 58, 83)

The Metropolitan Museum of Art, Crosby Brown Collection of Musical Instruments, 1889 (Pages 43, 45, 49)

The Metropolitan Museum of Art, Gift of R. Thornton Wilson, 1943 (Page 61)

Picture Collection, New York Public Library (Pages 42, 53)

The American Record Guide (Page 74)

Colbert Artists Management, Inc. (Page 10)

Hurok Concerts, Inc. (Page 32)

SBN: 531–01844–x

Library of Congress Catalog Card Number: 79-115773

Printed in the United States of America

Contents

The Flute

Jean-Pierre Rampal, contemporary flutist.

Prelude

You probably could not select a more romantic musical instrument to play than the flute. It is an instrument for all seasons. To hear its lovely liquid tones out of doors in the first days of spring is one of life's rarest treats. Few experiences equal that of playing a flute in the rustling shade of a spreading tree on a sunny knoll in summer. But when the land shimmers with full-moon silver, then that also seems the best time to play a flute—especially at harvesttime, when the moon rises as a huge, tawny disk pushing through dark, scudding clouds. Even indoors in dreariest winter the flute can be listened to for hours. It is an instrument close to nature, and one for all persons who respect the natural life.

The flute is a charming solo instrument, ideally suited to the average room, but it never is lost in a concert hall. With an orchestra, it frequently has important solo passages. There is plenty of good music for the flute. More has been written for it than for any other instrument except the piano and the violin.

This book will not tell you how to play the flute. You will need a good teacher for that—the best you can find. But it will give you a good deal of knowledge of your instrument: what it is and how its sound is made; where it came from and who its early inventors and makers were. Some of the details of present-day manufacture will be explained. You will be introduced to composers for the flute; you will make the acquaintance of notable concert flutists and jazz, folk, and rock performers on the flute.

You will find out how to enjoy concerts more and appreciate the role of the player in a symphony orchestra. You will read how best to care for your instrument. If you wish to delve deeper into flute lore, there is a list of books suggested for further reading and reference. A short list of flute recordings is also included, for a good way to learn your instrument and its musical possibilities is to listen to good professional flutists.

1. The Flute

The flute is a high-pitched member of the wind instrument family. The word "flute" is derived from the Latin word "*flatus*," which means "blowing" or "breathing." Wind instruments popularly are divided into two general classes: woodwind and brass. In all of them, air is used to make sound.

Among the woodwind instruments are the flute, the clarinet, the piccolo, the recorder, the flageolet, the fife, the oboe, the bassoon, the double bassoon, the saxophone, and the English horn, which is a large instrument similar to an oboe.

In the brass branch of the wind family are the trumpet, the cornet, the French horn, the trombone, the tuba, and the bugle.

Originally, classification of wind instruments was based on the material of which they were made. The woodwinds, except for the saxophones, were once constructed of wood; the brasses truly were made of brass. Now, however, woodwinds mostly are made of metal—stainless steel, nickel plate, silver plate, silver, or gold—and also of ivory, glass, ebonite (a hard vulcanized rubber), or plastics. Today you may even see flutes that are made of platinum. Brass instruments may now be made of silver, copper, ivory, animal horn, plastic—or even wood.

The basis of all wind instrument construction is a narrow

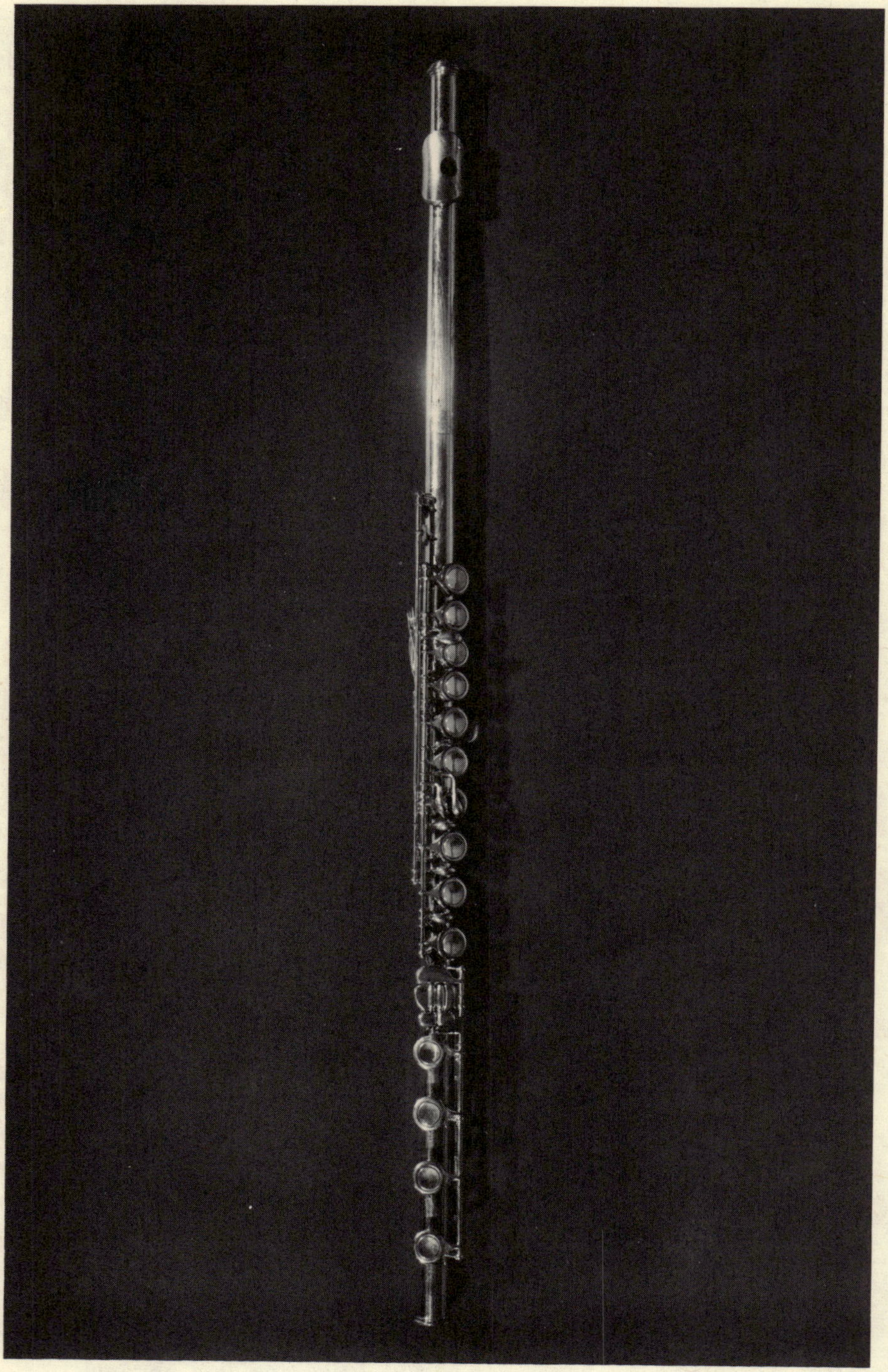

An American transverse flute made by Dayton C. Miller, Cleveland, Ohio, 1904–05.

tube. Woodwind tubes are short and straight. Brass tubes are long, are coiled into loops to make them manageable, and are usually flared into a bell shape at one end.

The flute is a pipe whose sides are pierced with holes, either open or capped by padded keys. It is played by blowing directly through or onto a mouthpiece without the added help of a reed.

A flute is classified according to which one of three mouthpieces it has. The most primitive is simply the open end of a tube, against which the flute player blows obliquely. This kind of mouthpiece is found on the ancient panpipe, or syrinx—a row of tubes graduated in length and bound together with the mouthpieces in an even row. It is played by blowing obliquely across the open mouthpiece ends of the tubes. You can understand how this mouthpiece works by blowing across the mouth of an empty soda bottle. Aside from the panpipes, flutes that are played in a vertical position, through one end, are equipped with whistle, or fipple, mouthpieces. A fipple mouthpiece is a built-in mouthpiece with a slot that shapes the air blown through it. Some people say that the word "fipple" comes from an Old Norse word, *flipi*; it means a "horse's lip," which the mouthpiece resembles.

The flute mouthpiece most used today is a simple hole cut into the side of the instrument near its head end. With such a mouthpiece, the flute must be held horizontally, parallel to the player's lips, at a right angle to his head and face, and usually extended to his right side. Because of the position in which it is held, this type of flute is called a cross, or transverse, flute, from *trans*, meaning "across," and *vertere*, a Latin word meaning "to turn."

The common transverse flute is a short cylindrical tube, usually of some kind of metal. Closed at one end, it is 26⅜ inches long, has a ¾-inch inside diameter, or bore, and is in three jointed sections. Student flutes are generally silver- or nickel-plated. The common professional model, however, is usually solid sterling silver.

The open-end section, called the *foot joint,* is the shortest; it measures 5⅛ inches, including its sleeve, which fits into the middle section, called the *body*. The closed-end section, the *head,* is 8¾ inches long; it fits onto the body section, which is 14½ inches in length, including its sleeve.

Wrapped halfway around the head section, about 1½ inches from its free end, is a convex oval mouthpiece of metal, about 2 inches long; in its center is an elliptical, or oval, hole, measuring about ½ or ⅜ of an inch. It is sometimes called the *embouchure* (pronounced om-boo-*shoor*), but that term more often refers to the way in which a flute player blows against the hole's edge in order to get a tone from the instrument.

In playing the keyed flute, all the fingers and the left thumb are used to push down round, lidlike padded keys onto the instrument's sixteen tone holes. The right thumb serves to support the instrument. Most keys remain in an open position until moved by the fingers. Some keys are manipulated directly; others, not in easy reach of the fingers, are operated by remote control—by touching small levers shaped somewhat like the heads of golf clubs or spoons. Thirteen of the keys are in the body of the tube, the midsection; the other three keys are in the foot joint, the open-end section, farthest from the player's mouth.

Not all of the keys remain in the open position, however. In addition to the twelve "open keys," there are four "closed keys," so called because their tone holes, unlike the others, are normally closed. In contrast to the open keys, these keys—

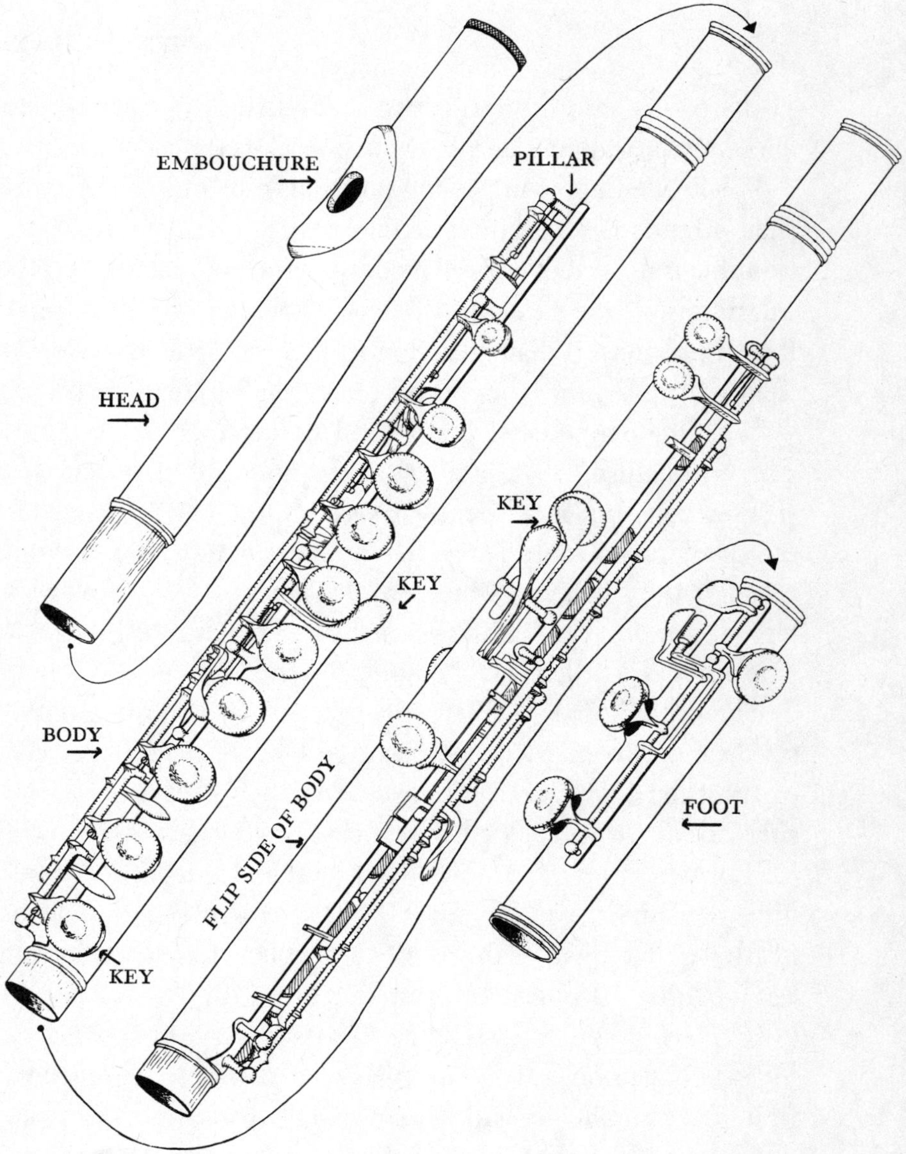

The three sections of the flute, showing key mechanism on both sides of the body.

D-sharp, G-sharp, and the two "trill keys"—are pressed to open, rather than close, their tone holes.

When the flute is in playing position, nine of its keys, with their attendant tone holes, are along the top of the mid section, beginning about eight inches from the mouthpiece and extending to the midsection's end. Each of the first eight tone holes has a diameter that is only a little bit smaller than that of a dime; the ninth hole is smaller than the others —about the diameter of a pea—and stands apart from them. The mechanism that controls it is not directly over this smaller hole, but is a lever that stands close to the lineup of large holes. On some flutes, five of these keys have holes cut through their centers, which can be covered by the player's finger cushions. Such flutes are called "French model flutes." The others are called "covered-hole flutes."

The other four keys of the midsection—two of them dime-sized, and two of them pea-sized trill keys—are on the side of the tube that faces the player. The trill keys are side by side, the first one located 6⅝ inches from the mouthpiece. Of the two larger, or thumb, keys of these four, one lies behind the blind key (actually a lever, as there is no hole beneath it) that operates the small topside key; the other thumb key is behind the fourth key from that blind key.

In playing position, the three keys of the open-end, or foot-joint, section usually are placed so that the one farthest from the tube's lower end faces obliquely forward, away from the player; the other two, which are in line, face obliquely backward, toward the player.

How does a flute make its particular sound?

Any sound—all sound—is the sensation of hearing a person gets from the reaction of his ears' auditory nerves to vibrations carried in the air or in water.

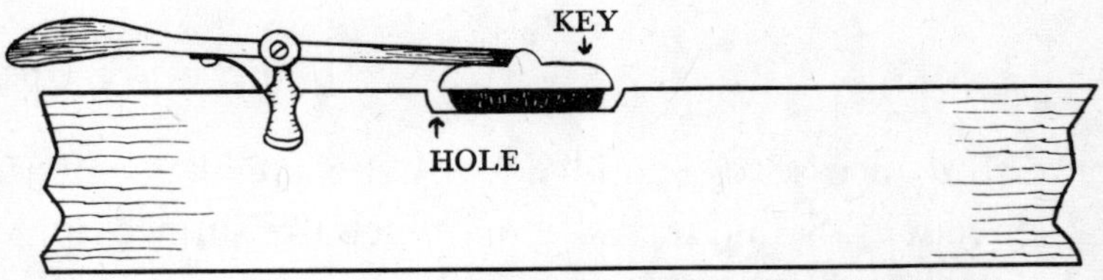

CLOSED POSITION OF FLUTE KEY

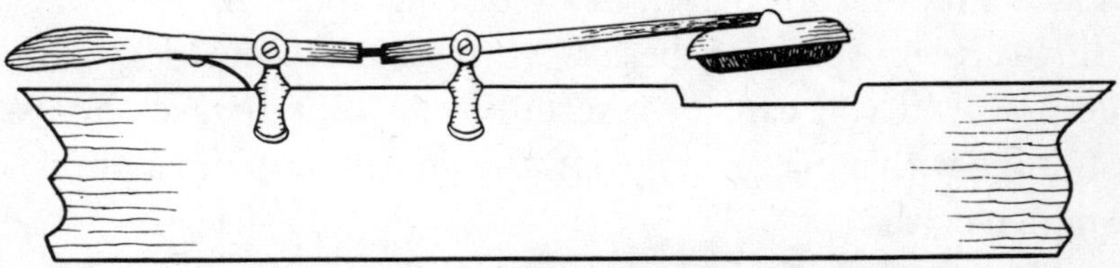
OPEN POSITION OF FLUTE KEY

Sound begins as vibration, which is the very fast back-and-forth movement in space of any thing, or any element, against which some outside force has been applied. This vibration is often invisible. To understand about vibration—actually, to see it—anchor, with one hand, the tip of the blade of a silver dinner knife at a table's edge, so that the knife extends out from it. Now pluck the knife's handle sharply with your other hand. The knife will shake vigorously up and down and make a humming sound. In other words, it vibrates from the force you have applied to it.

This vibration makes sound because it in turn is exerting force on the air around the knife and on the table under it.

The disturbance sends sound waves out in regular patterns in all directions. Sound waves go out much like surface ripples made when a pebble is dropped into a pool of water. But sound waves spread in *all* directions, not just as circles spreading out from a central point on a flat surface, and they are invisible. As they reach your ears your auditory nerves react and you hear the vibrations as sound.

While you cannot see sound, you can feel the vibrations that make it by lightly touching an operating television set, a radio, or a record player, or by placing your fingers to your throat as you speak or, better yet, to that of your dog as he growls. And you can see a recording of sound waves by examining with a magnifying glass the grooves cut into a phonograph record.

The sound of a wind instrument—either woodwind or brass —is produced when the air column within its tube is disturbed, so that the force of air entering the tube from outside sends lengthwise vibrations down through it toward the open end. In brass instruments the disturbing air comes into the tube through the player's vibrating lips, placed against a dome-shaped mouthpiece of metal. In a woodwind that uses a reed, or reeds, in its mouthpiece, the air within the tube is agitated by vibration of the reeds when the player blows on them. To see for yourself the vibrating-reed method—as in the clarinet, oboe, bassoon, and saxophone—stretch a good-sized blade of grass between your rigid, pressed-together thumbs and their heels. Blow vigorously against the blade's edge; the grass will vibrate and make a shrill squeal.

The sound of flute woodwinds is begun by blowing against an opening in the tube, either at one end or in its side. Some instruments of the flute group, such as the recorder, have a mouthpiece; air blown into it is formed into a concentrated

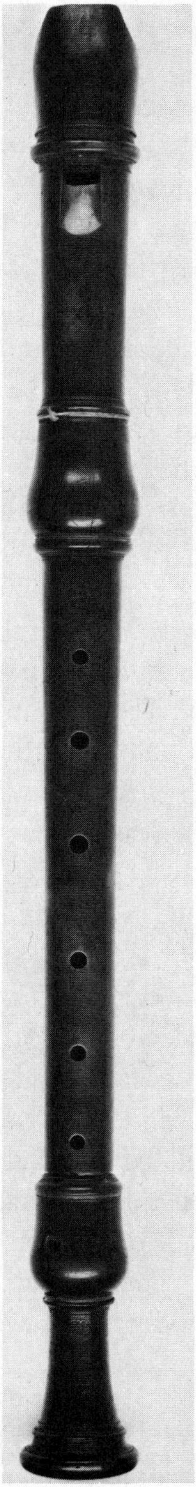

Recorder.

stream that is sent against the edge of a hole cut into the tube's side. The transverse flute has no such mouthpiece; the air is blown directly across the side opening, the embouchure, in a flat stream made by shaping the lips. This air force sometimes is referred to as the *air reed*. When it breaks against the sharp outer edge of the opening, this air is set into a flutter; it causes the stationary column of air within the tube to pulse and vibrate down the tube's length. This action generates a sound, called an edge tone, pitched in proportion to the length of the tube.

When the tube's column of air is long, its vibrations are slow, and a low tone results. When the column is short, the vibrations speed up and there is a high tone. You can observe this for yourself by setting up a kind of panpipe with soda bottles, each holding water at a different level. The bottle with the most water will have the least amount of air space—the shortest column of air—and will make the highest note when you blow across the bottles' neck openings. The bottle with the most air space, and the least water, will make the lowest tone.

To understand how shortened vibrating length affects pitch (the highness or lowness of a tone), take a long, flat stick—a yardstick will do nicely—and hold it firmly with about one-fourth of its length on a table at its edge, and the other three-fourths extending out into space. Bend down the free end of the stick and let it go. It will vibrate noisily. Listen to the tone of its vibrations. It will be low, because the stick is vibrating slowly. Now shorten the vibrating length a bit and repeat your action. The tone from the vibrations will be higher, because they are faster. The shorter you make the extended length, the faster the vibrations will be, and the higher their sound.

Lower-pitched sound waves have their peaks farther apart, while higher-pitched ones have peaks closer together. Changes in pitch do not alter the *height* of sound waves, but loudness of the sound does. Loud sound waves have higher peaks and lower valleys. We call that loudness *amplitude*. You can increase the amplitude of your extended vibrating yardstick by striking it harder. Note that while you have made the sound louder, the speed of the vibrations—that is, their frequency—remains the same.

The tone holes cut into the sides of the flute enable the scientific principle of the shortened vibrating column to be applied to this instrument. With all its holes closed, the flute makes its lowest note, because the vibrating air column that is captured within the tube must travel its entire length before escaping. The air column then is as long as it can be, and its vibrations are slow. They make a low sound. When the hole farthest from the mouthpiece is uncovered, the pitch is raised, because now the air escapes sooner, through the opened hole, so shortening the air column's vibrating length. As other holes are opened one by one, advancing toward the mouthpiece, the pitch becomes higher and higher, for the air column is being shortened by the progressive shortening of the escape distance; the sound waves go out the first hole they come to.

Opening the notes of a flute one by one and blowing normally result in its lowest octaves, with half tones. To get more tones from the instrument, the player resorts to what is called overblowing. The term is somewhat misleading, because this method of increasing a flute's range depends not so much on greater *power* of blowing, but rather on the player's pulling his lips in tighter, reshaping them so that the column of air passing through them will be more compressed.

To play notes that are not possible to achieve simply by shortening or lengthening the tube, flute players use what is known as cross-fingering. In cross-fingering, a tone hole is left open in a series of closed ones. Sound waves within a flute's tube are longer as the air column is longer, but cross-fingering shortens the sound waves slightly by opening a supplementary escape hole ahead of the main one, thereby allowing *some* of the vibrating air to get away before reaching the intended main exit—the first open hole beyond the closed section. A point of no vibration is created by this irregularity, which makes a different note than if the closed holes were all together in a row and *all* the vibrating air had to wait for escape until it completely passed the closed-hole section.

The standard modern flute is a C instrument—that is, it sounds a C as its lowest note. This flute is weak in upper harmonics, or overtones. Very little energy goes into coloring the tone, which therefore sounds almost transparent.

The normal concert flute has a range of three octaves with chromatic semitones, or half tones, from middle C upward. The lowest octave is slightly rough; it has a thick, velvety tone easily overwhelmed by other instruments. The middle octave is sweet, smooth, and limpid. The third, or top, octave is brilliant, birdlike, and penetrating. Its two highest semitones are almost impossible to play softly.

The alto flute is a G instrument, pitched one fourth lower than the standard flute; its lowest note is a G. It is sometimes, though incorrectly, called a bass flute, or a bass flute in G. It was especially in vogue during the eighteenth and early nineteenth centuries. It has a low, haunting tone that many players prefer to the higher one of the regular orchestral flute.

A true bass flute reaches a full octave below the ordinary flute. Bass flutes have been seen from time to time during

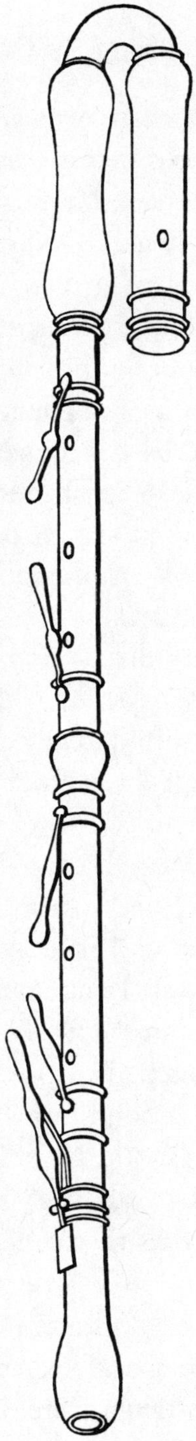

A bass flute of the eighteenth century.

the past two hundred years. Because a modern mechanism makes it possible to control the far-apart holes that are necessary in such long instruments, several have been constructed in recent times. In 1910, an Italian flutist named Albisi devised one that he called an Albisiphone; it was bent so that the mouth hole was in a crosswise position, while the tube was vertical. A true bass flute, introduced in 1932 by the English firm of Rudall Carte Ltd., of London, had a straight-across head, but the rest of the tube dropped diagonally; a projecting crutch, fitted over the player's thigh, took the instrument's weight off his arms. In 1953, Thomas Ogilvie, a pipe-organ expert of Los Angeles, California, invented a genuine bass flute that is 53 inches long and weighs 2¾ pounds.

The flute's nearest woodwind relatives are the piccolo, the recorder, the flageolet, the ocarina, the fife, the nose flute, whistles, the flute pipes of organs; the *nay* of Arabia, Persia, and Turkey; the ancient Egyptian *ma't*; and the panpipe, or syrinx.

The piccolo is really a small flute without the tailpiece, or foot joint, that gives the concert flute its three lowest keys. The piccolo's Italian name is *flauto piccolo*, or "little flute." It is one half the size of a concert flute and is pitched an octave higher. The piccolo's music sounds an octave higher than the written notes. It is the highest-pitched instrument of a band or orchestra. The piccolo's higher tones are shrill and penetrating, but its lower tones are weak. The technique of playing the flute and the piccolo is essentially the same. The third flute player in a symphony orchestra frequently doubles on the piccolo.

The recorder is a sort of half brother to the flute. After centuries of useful life the recorder fell into a decline, but it has been revived again in our time. It is a straight flute, held

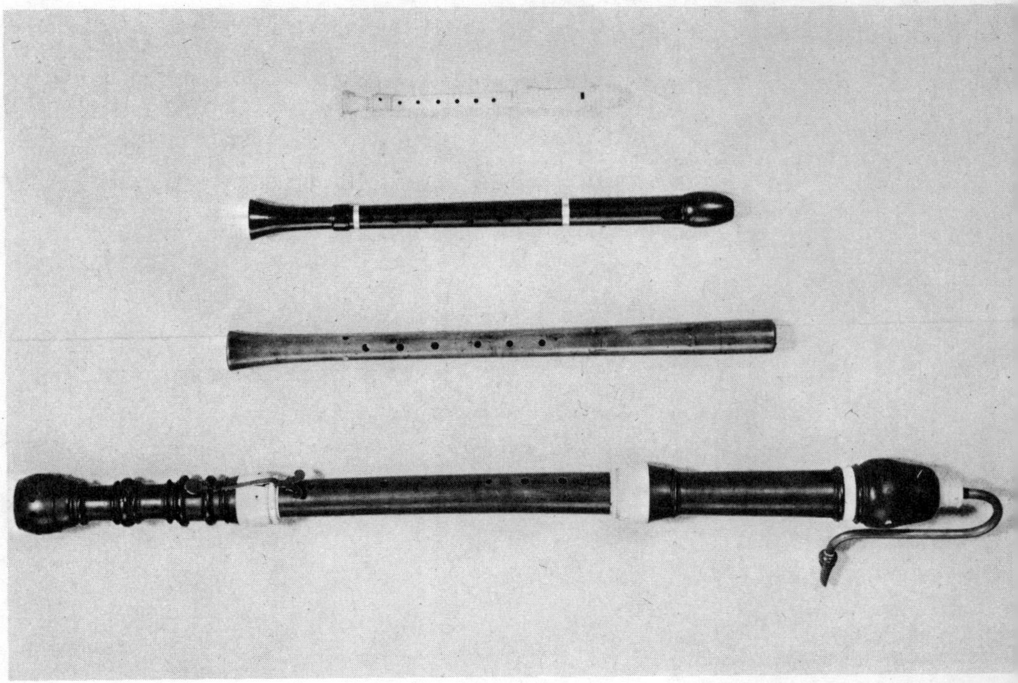

A family of recorders; reading from the top:
Soprano (ivory, eighteenth century)
Alto (wood, twentieth century)
Tenor (wood, sixteenth century)
Bass (wood, seventeenth century)

Flageolets:
Double (early nineteenth century)
Single (late nineteenth century)
Triple (eighteenth century)

vertically in playing, and blown through the end. The recorder is often called a beaked flute because it has a fipple mouthpiece through which the air enters. The French flageolet is a small-sized recorder; its chief difference is a smaller bore, which makes it more difficult to play than a recorder. There are double flageolets—with two tubes and a single mouthpiece.

The recorder, inexpensive and easier to learn than a flute, has eight tone holes—one each for the three middle fingers of each hand, one for the left little finger, and one for the right thumb. There are five common sizes of recorders. The descant is the usual one, with a range of two octaves, starting from C above middle C. Experienced players usually choose the treble recorder—a fifth below the descant—or the tenor, an octave below.

The quaintest of the flute's relatives is the Italian ocarina, a vaguely bird-shaped flute usually made of clay or porcelain. It has eight finger holes. The name comes from the Italian word oca, meaning "goose." The instrument may have received its name from its sound, or possibly from its shape.

The fife, pitched between the concert flute and the piccolo, was developed as an instrument to be played with a drum for soldiers on the march or on the battlefield. The military

Fife and drum of the French Infantry in the eighteenth century.

band began with the fife. The name is from the German word *pfeife,* meaning "tube" or "pipe." It originally came from the Middle Latin word *pipare,* which means "to cheep" or "to chirp."

The nose flute is just what its peculiar name implies: this flute is blown through a nostril, the left one, rather than by mouth.

2. *You as a Flutist*

The flute is a more difficult instrument than either the clarinet or the saxophone, but it can be mastered by almost any young student who has musical ability and a will to try. It is a fast-moving instrument that requires a quick player. Starting to learn it when you are young is a help. Some previous experience in playing a recorder is an advantage. Persons with especially faulty occlusion—the meeting of the upper and lower teeth—or those who have front teeth missing will not do well with the flute.

In buying a flute, bear in mind that the cheapest instrument can sometimes turn out to be the most expensive. Every flute is handsome—beautifully designed, wonderfully proportioned—but tones vary greatly. Good flutes are expensive.

To be a flutist of any sort, you must like music very much, and you must be sure that the flute is the instrument you really want to play. Otherwise, there is not much point in even beginning to study it.

Besides the desire to play, you will need a down-to-earth willingness to work and an ability to concentrate, and you will need patience, self-reliance, and self-discipline.

While it is being played, the transverse flute is held at an almost 90-degree angle to the face. The player holds the instrument under his lower lip, against his chin, as he blows across

Contemporary flutist Elaine Shaffer in recital.

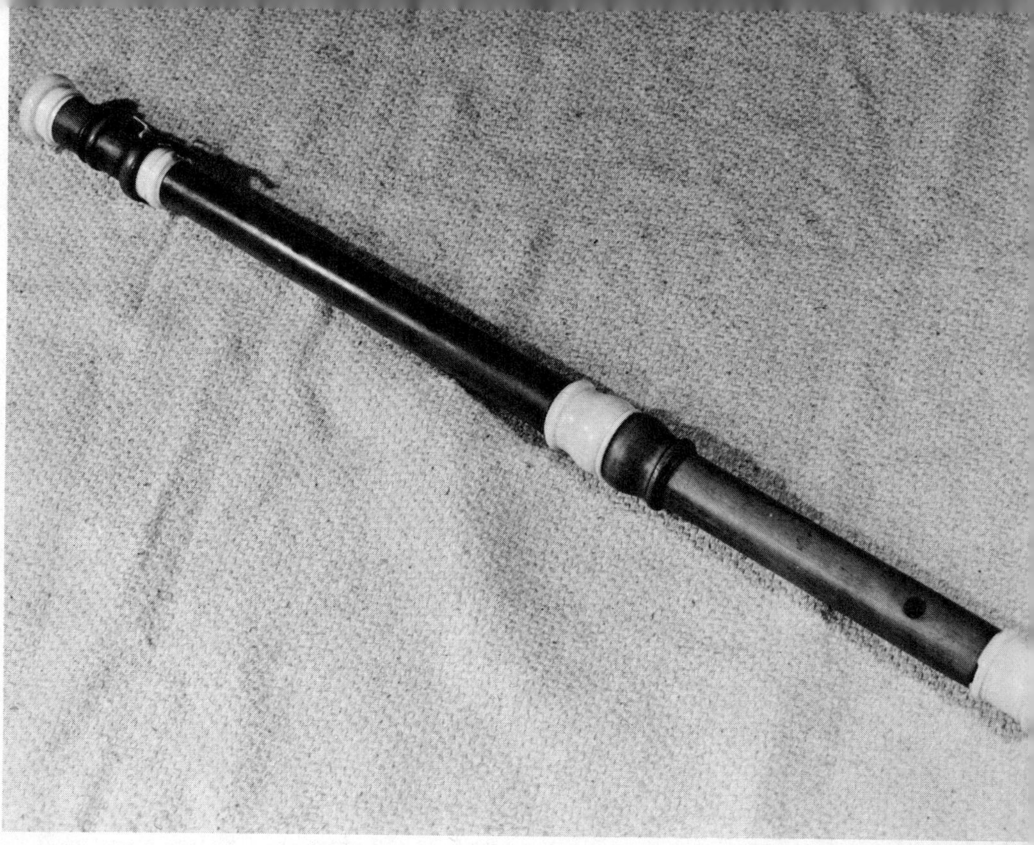

Early eighteenth-century flute of boxwood, with only one key (silver) and ivory fittings.

the mouth hole, or embouchure. As a flutist, you will have to get used to holding your arms in one position for long periods of time. But you will develop stronger muscles as you work along.

Especially strong hands and fingers are not necessary; they must, however, be supple. The flute has an established set of fingerings—there are no two or three ways of playing the same note. In fact, very few notes can be played by using auxiliary fingerings, and this can be done only for very specific purposes.

While it is true that the fingers always rest on, or touch, the same keys, the high register of the flute depends on "combination" fingerings: in order to pass from one tone to the other in this register, the flute player may have to synchronize the action of three, four, five, or more fingers.

You can make your fingers more limber and responsive by regular practice of the following simple exercise. Close your fingers so that their tops rest on the fleshy cushions at their bases. Then slowly extend each finger, one at a time, while keeping the others clenched shut.

In order to develop finger control, hold your extended fingers all together and then separate them from each other, one by one. If you study typing in school, that use of your hands, fingers, and forearms will benefit you in playing the flute.

You will need a feeling for tempo, or the speed of music, and tone color, or timbre. Tone color is the quality of a tone: thin, thick, light, dark, sharp, dull, smooth, rough, warm, cold, velvety, fuzzy, or rounded, for instance. Your playing will be flat and uninteresting until you have learned to weave color into your tones.

You will also need a good sense of pitch, for the flute is built in such a way that it must be kept in tune by the physical force of the player. Every note of a flute must be tempered by the way the player uses his breath and lips. With a flute, too, there is constant danger of the pitch's being altered by temperature changes. Therefore you must be able to recognize the difference in pitch—the distance between tones that is called an interval. If at first you have trouble with this skill, do not give up. Your ear can be trained to find the notes you seek. One good way of practicing ear training is to try to identify the tones of the ordinary sounds around you—a bird's song, a church bell, a factory or a train whistle, an automobile's horn.

The flute student finds his greatest technical difficulty in conquering the embouchure. This word for the mouthpiece

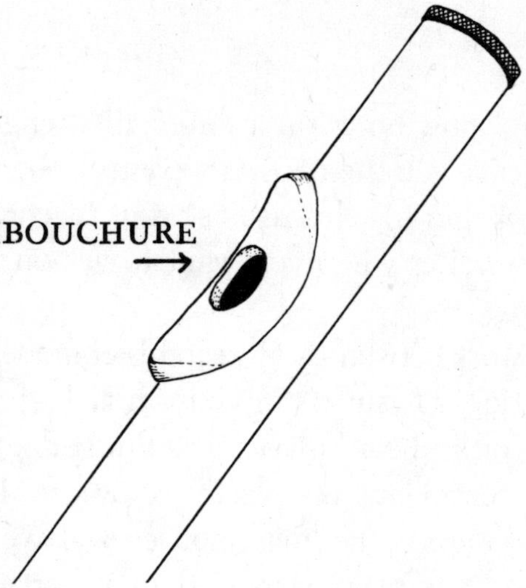

The embouchure.

of a transverse flute is also used to mean the way of applying the lips, and sometimes the tongue, to any wind instrument's mouthpiece.

Anyone can put a flute to his lips, blow some air into it, and get a tone of sorts. But only a real player can get an accurately pitched tone that has the quality needed to make beautiful music. With a transverse flute you do not simply push down the right keys and blow. That method will not get you the right tones at all. In order to make them on this type of flute, you must develop great control of your mouth muscles. You need to blow with the lips correctly shaped in certain ways, and held just firmly enough in those positions so that exactly the right amount of air is blown out each time at exactly the right pressure. *Everything* has to be right. Otherwise, your tones will definitely be off. In a broad sense a whistler uses embouchure control when he varies pitch by changing the shape of his lips and tongue in whistling.

The practice of long, slow notes on a flute will strengthen your embouchure and give you the necessary control. Remember this whenever you begin to rebel against your teacher for keeping you at such exercises when you want to get on with practicing new fingerings.

A flute player must work constantly to keep his embouchure in good playing condition. He suffers more from lack of practice than does a string or keyboard player. If a flutist does not touch his instrument for weeks, his playing shows it. If he goes longer without practice, he may not even have the strength in his lip muscles to play for more than a short time.

If you are to become good on the flute, nothing beats practice. Practice a lot, but still, do not overdo it. Try to reach a nice balance between spending too much of your energy—and becoming exhausted and despairing—and sparing yourself too much and not making the headway you should. An hour of good practice a day will work wonders. Sometimes several short snatches of practice are better than one long, drawn-out session. Try both ways, then choose the style that suits you best. Be steady; try to practice at the same time each day. You cannot make up lost practice time by adding it to a future period.

Think of practice positively. Do not become a prisoner of your flute. Instead, make it a pleasant companion. Practice to improve your mutual performance, and when you practice, concentrate.

Ideally, you should be alone with your teacher during your lesson. Sometimes, if a student is quite young, it is a good idea for someone in the family to stand by during the lesson—with the teacher's permission, of course—for the purpose of noting mistakes and weak points as the teacher finds them, and then seeing that they are corrected at practice. But remember, the teacher is the important person to heed and to please. His job is to help you all he can. Be wise in your choice of a teacher. If you simply want to play the flute for pleasure, the sort of instructor who customarily trains only concert artists is not for you. On the other hand, if you want to play professionally, do not select a teacher who knows little or nothing about the concert field.

Try not to repeat mistakes, and do not learn things wrong. It takes much longer to unlearn something and relearn it another way than it does to learn it right in the first place. Be thorough. Slow practice will result in quick playing. Be critical of yourself; judge every tone as though someone else were making it. If you will practice once in a while before a large mirror, you can see the positions of your fingers and lips and your general stance, and be sure that they are correct.

Learn to read music as you would a newspaper or a book. So that your musical outlook will be broadened, make it an aim to learn many different kinds of musical pieces, and not just classical concert numbers. Do not hesitate to play social and popular music on your flute—pop, rock, folk rock, jazz, and show tunes. This sort of music will let you perform freely and help you to develop a relaxed, enjoyable attitude toward performing. You will learn to play by ear, and because popular music need not be so strictly interpreted, you will pick up ways of improvising that are not used in the classical field. Moreover, this kind of playing will make music a part of your everyday life and not something that is confined only to music lessons and practice sessions.

Rely on your teacher's advice at all times, but do not fail to question those things you do not understand or do not agree with. In music, as in every other field of endeavor, it is the inquiring mind that becomes the strongest. Whatever is taught you, make it your own. But test what you learn, to see whether it is in harmony with what you believe in your heart. Everyone looks at music differently, and your viewpoint may be a perfectly good one.

Above all, bear in mind that, besides a great deal of hard work at technique, the flute requires of its player a romantic temperament—a bit of dash, and more than a little fire. Approach the flute with the same sense of joy that its music gives.

You will find that the flute can speak in all sorts of ways. Only one note at a time can be played on this instrument, but the musical effects that can be created by a skilled performer are almost unlimited. He can achieve sustained notes, both *diminuendo*—or diminishing—and *crescendo*—or increasing. With ease and rapidity he can run standard scales of eight tones (diatonic scales) and those progressing by half tones (chromatic scales). He can dash off *arpeggios*—playing the notes of a chord rapidly, one after the other, ripplingly. And he can play the arpeggios either *legato*—in a smooth, connected manner—or *staccato*—in briefly held notes detached from each other. He can bring forth notes that leap and turn, shake and tremble, dance, and perform all sorts of musical acrobatics. Rapid staccato passages are easy for a player who has mastered double and triple tonguing on a flute.

You may not wish to become a professional flutist. But no matter how far you care to go with your playing, the flute will bring you a warm, intimate pleasure that few other musical instruments are able to offer. Learn to play the flute as though it were an added part of yourself. Let it speak with love and understanding.

3. *The Flute's History*

Throughout its long existence the flute has been associated with magic and mysterious rites. Among primitive peoples it is credited with all sorts of secret powers. Flute playing is counted on to bring rain and also to stop a storm. A flutist's notes are supposed to strike down an enemy, or cause a cow to give more milk, or a pig to produce many young. Flute music supposedly protects a person from danger in raging rivers or floods, and from fevers, delirium, and death. It is good insurance against tigers, rats, demons, and the doldrums.

In the days of the Aztecs, slaves played flutes as they were sent to have their hearts cut out by high priests in the sacrificial festivals to the god Tezcatlipoca. So that their souls would be preserved, the unfortunate young slaves customarily broke a bone flute on each step of the fateful temple as they ascended it to meet the priests at the top.

Often, when archeologists have excavated ancient ruins, they have found a flute at the side of a mummy or a skeleton. It was probably placed there as a charm to guarantee a new life after death. The Todas, an East Indian tribe, do not make or play flutes. The instruments are fashioned by neighboring tribesmen, however, and are used as amulets for the Toda dead, in order to guarantee fortunate rebirth.

Some of the American Indians formerly used the flute in

American Indian flutes; reading from the top:
Sioux love flute
Alaskan vertical flute of carved slate
Jibaros (Ecuador) cross or transverse flute
Bottom left: Guatemalan clay whistle
Bottom right: Choco (Colombia) panpipe

their fertility rites and dances, but it was best known among them as a lover's aid—something with which to impress and influence a girl. A young Cheyenne who was too bashful to ask his sweetheart to marry him might hide among the bushes close to a spring where the maiden went every morning for water. When his love appeared, he would play softly on his flute a little tune that he had made up for her ears alone. She would pretend not to notice, but would eventually find out who the player was. If she felt favorable to his suit, she would give a sign; he would then come out of his hiding place and soon the couple would be wed. If she was not interested, the

girl would let the young man go on playing every morning until finally, in sorrow and frustration, he would break his flute over his knee. Some other North American Indian tribes have also followed this courting custom.

In many primitive societies the nose flute is closely associated with magic. Nose breath is supposed to contain the soul, and therefore has more magic power than mouth breath.

The flute has a reputation as an instrument for singing nature's praises. Very likely this reputation comes in part from the flute's association with the pipes of Pan, who was the

Ancient Greece: detail from vase.

Panpipes.

mythological Greek god of fields, forests, wild animals, flocks, and shepherds. Pan appears in pictures as a droll fellow with a goat's legs and stubby tail; a naked torso; long, pointed ears; little sharp chin whiskers; and small curled horns.

Another name for the panpipe is the *syrinx*. More exactly, it is *syrinx polykalamos*, Greek for "syrinx with many canes." The word "syrinx" itself comes from a Semitic word that means "he hissed," or "he whistled."

According to a Greek myth, Syrinx was the name of a beautiful water nymph with whom Pan fell in love. Every time he tried to tell her of his devotion, she became frightened by his grotesque appearance and ran away. One day he pursued her through a wood to a riverbank. When, in alarm, she called out to her friends the water nymphs, they magically transformed Syrinx into a stand of tall reeds. When Pan reached out to embrace his love, he found only these reeds in his arms. He sighed in disappointment, and his breath, passing through the broken hollow reeds, made a sorrowful musical sound. Hearing this, Pan cut the reeds into different lengths, bound them together with the tendrils of a vine, and made the first wind instrument, which he named syrinx in memory of his lost love.

Panpipes are still played in Peru and Bolivia, in South America. A favorite Bolivian form is the twin panpipes—two sets of pipes fastened together by a long cord and played by two performers. Since each instrument has only half the notes of the scale—every other note is missing on each flute, and each has the notes the other lacks—the performers must follow each other's playing very closely in order to make a melody come out right. The Karenni of the Burmese backcountry have similar twin panpipes. The panpipes are also played in Eastern Europe, China, and Mongolia.

Flutes made of bird bone, and dating back to the Stone Age, have been discovered, yet no historian of musical instruments is sure where, when, how, or even why, the flute came into being.

Nearly every ancient race has been credited with its origin. The Chinese, the Japanese, the Etruscans, the Greeks, the Romans, and the Egyptians all have been thought to be the first flute makers. It is hard to know the truth of the matter, as primitive forms of the flute are found in widely separated parts of the globe.

When white men first landed in Africa, flutes and whistles

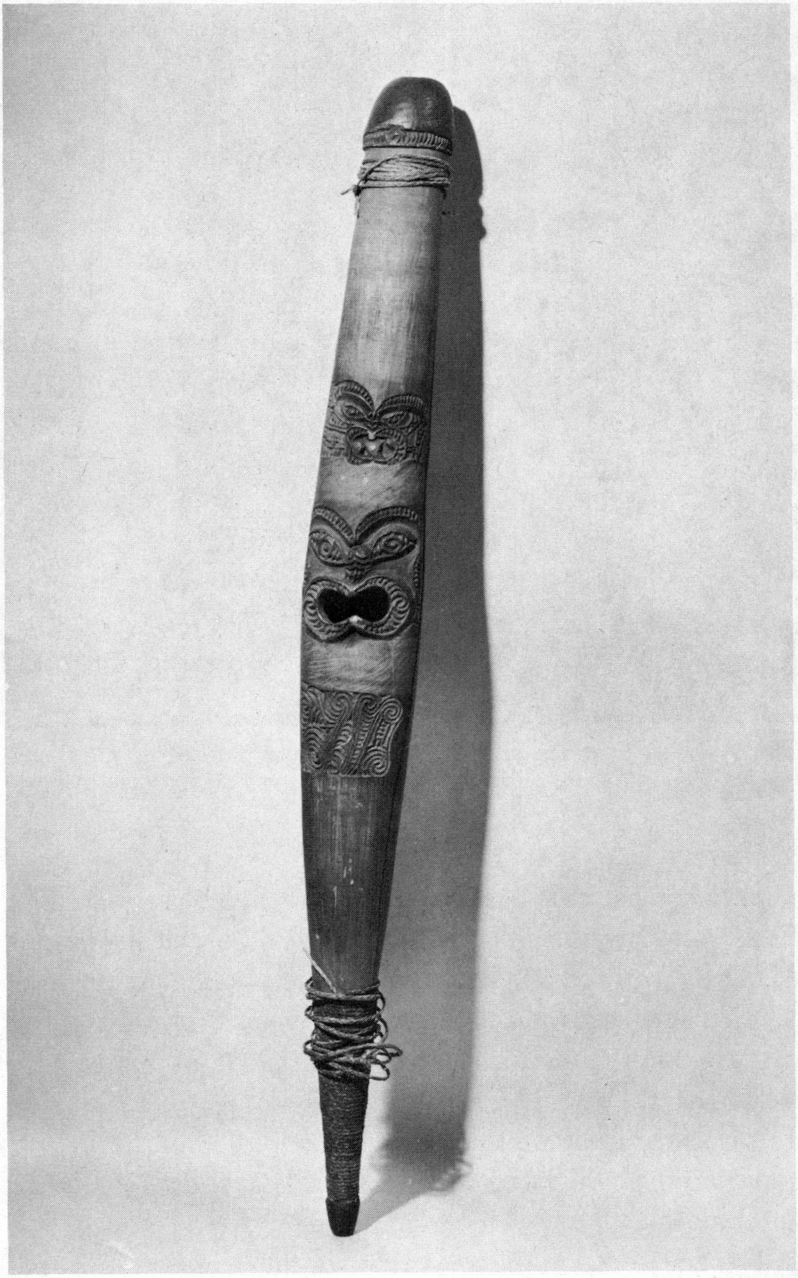

A two-piece flute from New Zealand.

China: ivory figurines showing girls playing transverse flute and panpipe.

were being played in the bush. Native flutes are played in Russia, in Australia and New Zealand, and on all the islands of the South Pacific. Mexicans play the *pito*, an Aztec flute; South American Indians have flutes whose form has been handed down from Inca ancestors. Eskimos in Alaska play native flutes.

It is widely believed that flutes first appeared in the Orient, and from there migrated to the Middle East and on to Greece and Italy.

There are enough different kinds of flutes on record in the Far East to give Orientals a strong basis for their claim of having the longest flute history. The Chinese boast that their flute, the *tsche*, originated in 2637 B.C. It is a transverse bamboo flute with a mouth hole on the side, at its center, flanked on each side by three finger holes. In the twelfth century B.C. came the Chinese *kuan hsiao;* in the ninth century B.C., the *ch'ih;* in the eighth century B.C., the *yuëh;* and later came the *yo* and the *ti*. The *ch'ih*, a transverse flute, is still played in China, usually in unison with a globular flute. A popular whistle flute of the Orient is the Chinese *t'ai p'ing hsiao*, which has six front holes, and above them one hole covered with a delicate membrane, which vibrates when the flute is

Chinese jade flute, with notch at one end to facilitate blowing.

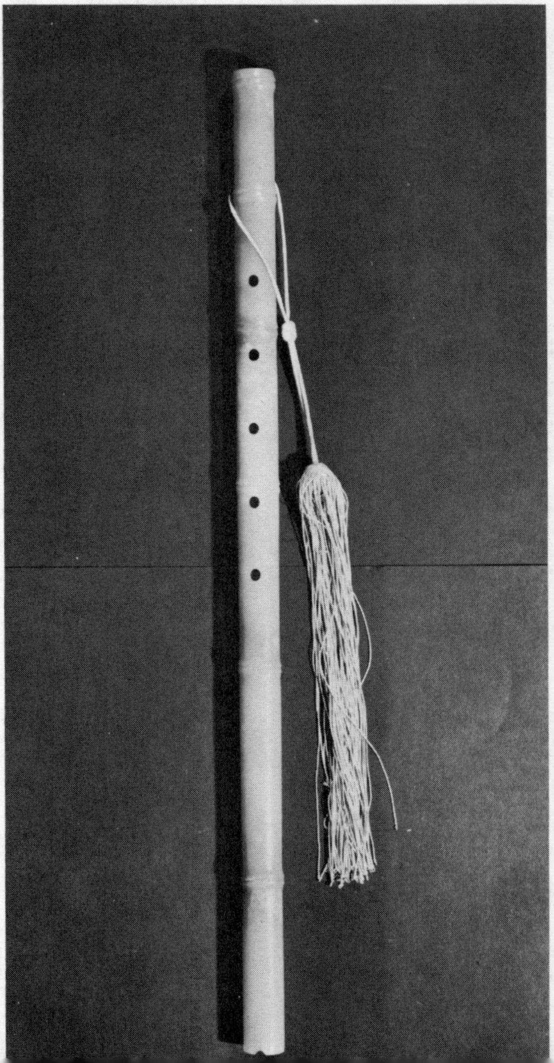

Japanese print by the artist Utamaro (1754–1806): flute girl at an inn.

played, and makes the tone somewhat nasal. In the high reaches of Tibet, herdsmen play a triple flute called a *gLingbu*. Oriental flutes are usually made of bamboo.

In about 2600 B.C., flutes were used in rituals in Mesopotamia, an ancient country lying between the rivers Tigris and Euphrates, where Iraq is now located. The first rulers of Mesopotamia were the Sumerians. Their name for the vertical flute was *ti-gi*. The syllable *gi* means "cane."

Assyria: relief showing ancient flutists and string players in the seventh century B.C.

The outstanding wind instrument of ancient India was a transverse flute called, in Sanskrit, the *vāṁsī*. It first appears on temple relief carvings of the first century A.D., at Sanchi in central India.

The Hindu divinity Krishna is said to have played the flute when he disguised himself as a cowherd to avoid being killed by his enemies. It is written that when Krishna's flute sounded, "the spirits were enchanted; the rivers paused and stopped flowing; the birds, halting in their flight, flew down and listened jealously; all the inanimate things under the sun grew brighter."

An early likeness of a vertical flute—about 4000 B.C.—has been found in Egypt. It is a picture on slate of a hunter playing a flute to lure game. This flute is called a *ma't*. Larger than our present-day concert flute, the *ma't* was cut from a piece of cane generally about three feet long and one half inch in diameter. There were from two to six finger holes near its lower end; some of these flutes had a thumbhole in back; there was no whistle head. This kind of flute is still played in Haiti, where it is called an *oban*.

Several ancient flutes have been found in Egyptian catacombs—underground chambers where the dead were buried—and a painting of seven flute players, made about 2000 B.C., was found in a pyramid at Gizeh. In the British Museum are paintings dating from about 1300 B.C., showing women playing the double flute at a festival in honor of the Egyptian god Ptah; the same kind of flute is still used by boatmen on the Nile River.

The ancient country of Etruria, on the northwestern coast of what is now the Italian peninsula, seems to have had flutes at a fairly early time. An excavation of an Etruscan tomb of the second century B.C., near Perugia, turned up an urn on

India: Krishna playing the flute, seventeenth-century carving in wood.

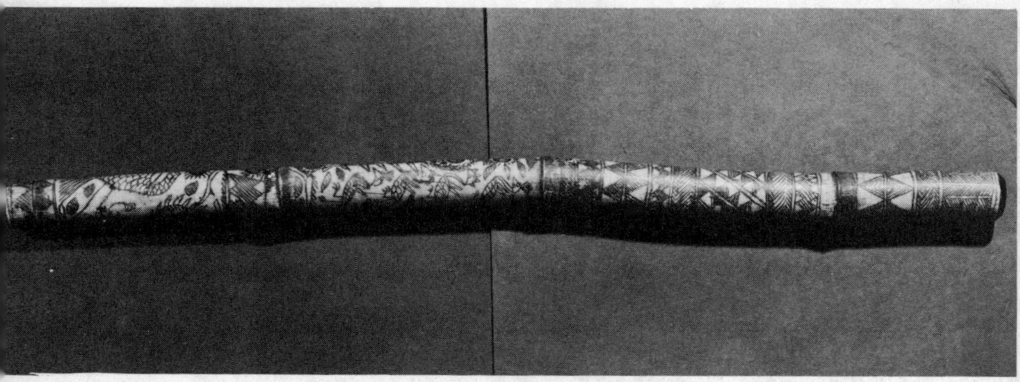

Egyptian vertical flute.

which is the sculptured head of a musician playing a transverse flute. It is the earliest representation of the flute yet found on the European continent.

The only evidence of a flute shown in early Greco-Roman times is a transverse flute stamped on a coin dated A.D. 169. Transverse flutes are mentioned, as *plagioi,* in Greek writings of about A.D. 800, and are shown in Greek miniatures of the tenth and eleventh centuries.

A popular relative of the Greek flute was the *aulos,* a woodwind rather like our oboe. The *aulos* was a single or double wooden pipe with a double reed mouthpiece. Originally it had three or four finger holes; later these were increased to as many as sixteen. Its music was shrill and exciting, like that of bagpipes. There were *auloi* ranging from bass to soprano. In annual music festivals, men competed to determine the finest *auloi* players; the winners became the highest paid musicians in the land.

It took so much power to blow the *aulos* that only males attempted it. The player wore across his mouth a leather band in which there were two holes just large enough for the reeds to pass through. This device gave regular pressure to the windswollen cheeks, which the player used as bellows. The Greeks called the leather band a *phorbeia;* the Roman name for it was *capistrum.* Similar blow bands were used in the East Indies, where an instrument like the *aulos* was played during the first thousand years before Christ.

The first tangible evidence of the flute's travels through middle Europe is a picture made around A.D. 1100 of a transverse flute. That picture is now in the National Museum at Budapest, Hungary.

In the Middle Ages there were two kinds of flutes: "cross flutes and flutes that you play straight," according to French fourteenth-century composer Guillaume de Machaut. The

Medieval Germany: concert by minstrels playing fiddle and transverse flute.

straight flute, given an Old French name, *flageol*, was a beaked flute, or recorder.

In the early seventeenth century there were seven sizes of *flageols*, ranging in length from nine inches to six feet eight inches. The big one was blown through a brass crook similar to that now used on a bassoon. Recorders in large groups appeared in concerts. One type had a nozzle of bone instead of the usual fipple mouthpiece; it led to a bulging chamber that held a sponge for absorbing the player's spittle.

The French also developed a one-handed flute, called either a *fluet* or a *galoubet*. It was a recorder with a very narrow bore and only three holes—two in front and one behind them—so that it could easily be played with one hand. The other hand beat on a small drum, or else plucked the thick gut strings of a zither. The one-hand flute still is found among the Basques of the Spanish and French Pyrenees.

In the later Middle Ages the center of flute activity was Germany, where the instrument was used mainly by soldiers. From there the flute spread across the rest of Europe.

At the beginning of the seventeenth century, which ushered in the Baroque period (about 1600–1750), a radical revolution in music occurred. A polyphonic style of playing, in which two or more melodies occur at the same time, was replaced by a monophonic style, in which one part is strongest. Because of this trend, only musical instruments with a very wide range of tone remained popular. Stringed instruments dominated the field, but the flute survived because it was needed to add zest to the string sounds. To meet the new demands on it, however, the flute had to undergo a few minor alterations. Its bore was changed from cylindrical to conical, a style that was kept for about two hundred years. And instead of four sections with as many as seven extra interchangeable parts, for adjusting pitch, the flute now had only two sections.

These changes made the instrument musically more versatile, but its greatest transformation came in 1808, when corrective tone holes were added. Eventually an entirely new system of keys and fingering was based on these additional holes, and the flute came into its own.

4. *Famous Flute Makers*

Until about 1660, no flute had more than six finger holes. That seemed to be enough, for at that time little fingers and thumbs were considered too weak and clumsy to be of use in playing.

But flutists finally became dissatisfied with the limited range of their instrument. Someone figured that maybe another tone hole down near the foot of the flute would improve matters. Since no finger was long enough to reach such a hole, the suggestion was made that perhaps some sort of lever could be rigged to open and close the hole; a little finger could be used to operate this device. At first, many people were against spoiling the lovely simple lines of the flute with something mechanical. But finally a Frenchman, whose name no one remembers, devised an acceptable arrangement that enabled the right little finger to work a closed key over a hole placed at some distance from the existing tone holes.

This was the first key any flute ever had—a D-sharp. It made the flute enormously more useful. Such a remote-control key had been used briefly on a flute back in 1413 in the Netherlands, and one had turned up again as a suggestion in 1636. Why had it taken so long for the flute to get its first really important improvement? The French, who were the best flute players, shrugged, and put the blame on the cloddishness of the Germans, who had long held a monopoly on flute making. The Germans answered back by saying they had to keep the flute simple so that the French could play it.

The remodeled flute was taken up by several French musical-instrument manufacturers, most of whom doubled as flute virtuosos. They included Louis Hotteterre, Michel de Labarre, Pierre Gabriel Buffardin, and Michel Blavet.

About twenty years after the flute received its first key, another major step forward was made when the cylindrical bore was replaced by a conical one. Most flutists then thought that this tapering of the inside of the tube toward its open end greatly improved the instrument's tone. The exact date of the changeover is unknown. The conical flute, however, was in use before the end of the seventeenth century; engravings of it appeared in 1699, in the first complete flute instruction manual ever published—by the flute-making firm of Hotteterres, established in 1650.

About 1722, the flute was lengthened so that two open keys could be added—one for C-natural, the other for C-sharp. Some players thought this an improvement; others disagreed. The change proved so unpopular that these keys were soon eliminated.

The Germans no longer made all the best flutes. A celebrated flute maker of the period was a Roman named Il Biglioni. Another was a Frenchman, F. Boie, an ancestor of J. F. Boie, the man who much later, in 1785, invented conical keys made of the soft metal pewter, instead of leather. These keys, over holes lined with silver, made excellent stops, but were so noisy that few flutists adopted them.

In 1726, a master flutist, Johann Joachim Quantz, added a second closed key—an E-flat—to the instrument's foot joint. This key enabled Quantz to use eighteen notes in the flute's

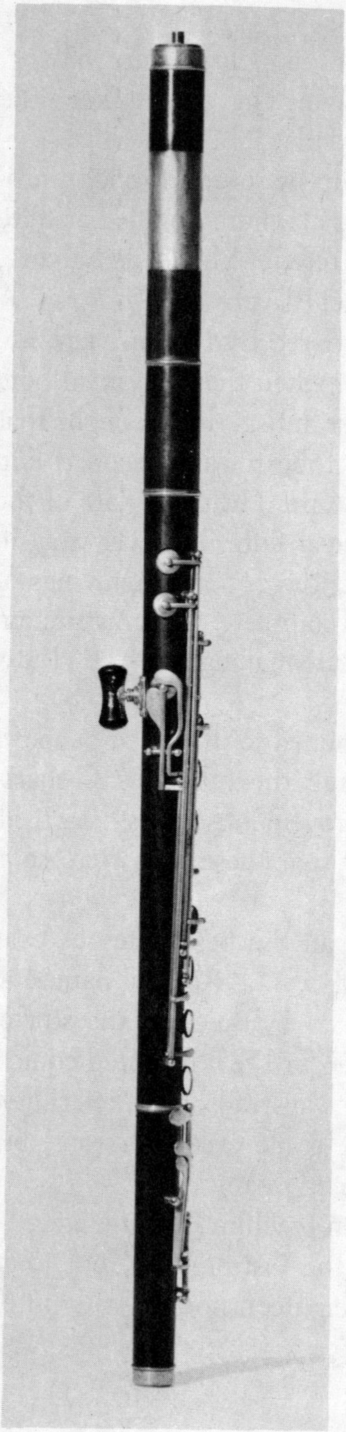

A conical flute made in New York City, about 1850.

Johann Joachim Quantz.

first octave, and twenty-seven in the second. Outside Germany, Quantz's key did not get much notice. His instrument was made of ebony, had a screw cork closing one end, and a circular embouchure almost half an inch in diameter.

By 1751, flute makers were turning out ungainly bass flutes, so long that the first, third, fourth, sixth, and seventh finger holes had to be closed by long, thin, awkward mechanical levers.

In 1774 came the greatest improvement in the flute since the D-sharp key—the addition of finger holes for the notes F-natural, G-sharp, and B-flat. At first, these holes were covered by closed keys, so that the player could use them or not, depending on how he felt or how skillful he was.

Early flute makers were hesitant about making changes in their instruments. It took over fifty years for the revival of the two foot-joint keys—C-natural and C-sharp—that had been added around 1722 and then abandoned. Florio, a famous flutist in an opera orchestra in London, reinvented these keys in about 1774. They worked so well that he kept a small curtain over the foot of his flute to prevent people from knowing how he produced these particular low notes. His daughter alone was entrusted with the secret, so that it would be kept in the family.

The next significant advance in the flute was the addition of a middle C-sharp hole, which made the flute into a chromatic instrument; now every note of the chromatic scale was provided for. Very few flutists liked the new holes, because their placement made them difficult to use in certain passages.

The problems of how to cover and uncover flute finger holes continued to bother both flutists and flute makers. There always seemed to be some revolutionary notion or device that promised to make things easier for the player's overtaxed fingers. Few of the ideas were workable.

The flute remained imperfectly constructed until 1808, when the Reverend Frederick Nolan of England, an amateur flute maker, invented the ring key, which permitted the addition of corrective holes. The ring key is a springing metal ring suspended over a regular open hole and connected by a lever with another key over an auxiliary, or helping, hole that is beyond reach of a playing finger. The auxiliary hole stays open and functions as a correction as long as the hole under the ring key is open. But when it is closed by pressing down on the

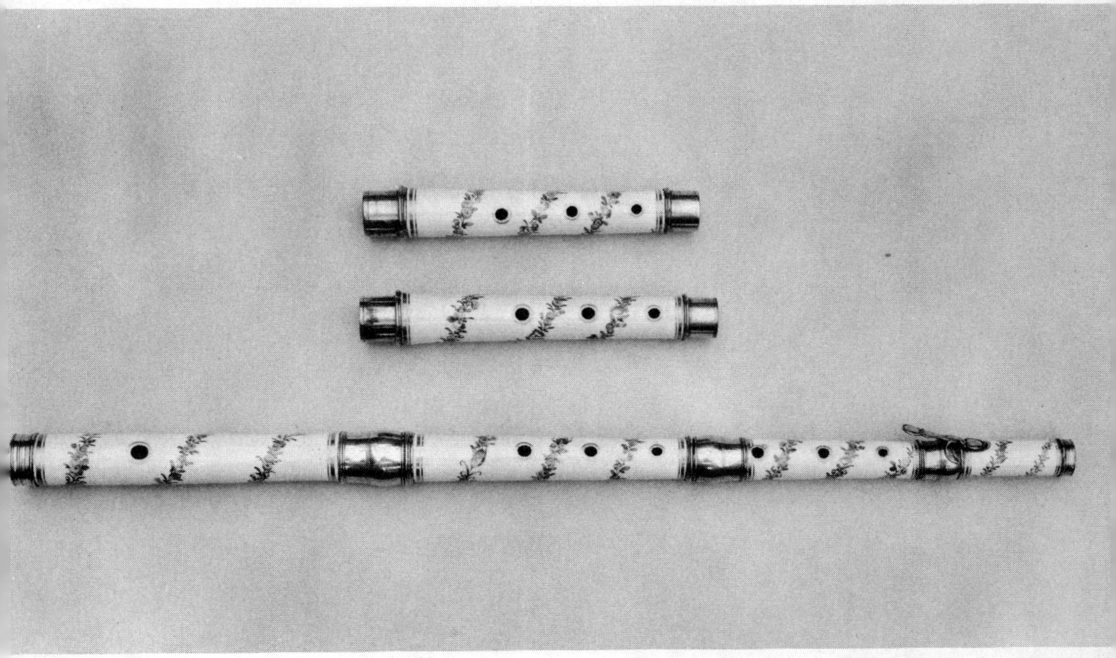

A porcelain flute, made in six sections in southern Germany, in the eighteenth century.

ring, the auxiliary hole also automatically closes, so that it does not interfere with lower holes.

In 1822, Charles Nicholson, a flutist then at the peak of his popularity, began making large-holed flutes of cocuswood. Interesting features of these instruments were an embouchure bushed with ivory, a metal-lined head joint furnished with a tuning slide and a screw cork, and on the tube's outside surface, various hollowed-out spots—some lined with sharkskin—to accommodate the joints of a player's fingers.

About this time, in the early nineteenth century, William Gordon, a former captain in the Swiss Guards of the French

Gordon's flute.

Early Boehm flute.

king Charles X, made a flute in which he used Nolan's ring key, but with tone holes in an entirely changed pattern, which he considered more practical. Gordon's system was inspired by the crude schemes of two other makers. They were Johann George Tromlitz, who did more than any other flute maker to bring into use the system of open keys employed today, and Dr. H. W. Pottgeiser, who in 1803 made a flute with holes placed more in keeping with the scientific principles of sound-making. The machinery of Gordon's flute was beautifully executed in steel by a Swiss watchmaker.

In 1831, Gordon met Theobald Boehm, the renowned principal flutist to the king of Bavaria, and the son of a prominent goldsmith. The two men exchanged friendly notes and letters; while he was supervising the building of his own newly invented flute, Gordon lived for nine months in Boehm's household in Munich, making use of Boehm's craftsmen and equipment and seeking his advice.

Soon afterward, in 1832, Boehm, who had been making flutes for twenty years, brought out a flute with an entirely new system of tone holes, keys, and levers. Boehm boasted that his new flute was much better than Gordon's, which he described as "false in its intonation—its machinery too complicated to be of any real use."

Nevertheless, Boehm was accused of stealing most of the ideas for his flute from Gordon. Boehm denied the charges and soon had a factory turning out his new flutes. They sold well.

For years the two flute makers carried on a bitter feud as they disputed which one had invented what we now know as the modern flute. Finally, Gordon went insane and died.

For a long time, music historians differed over whether Gordon or Boehm was first with the altered placement of

Theobald Boehm.

holes and the new fingerings that proved so successful that they have lasted to our time. Boehm had the reputation of using the ideas and methods of the flute makers who had preceded him, including some of the ideas of his teacher, Capeller. Many authorities at the time felt that Gordon had borrowed very little from Boehm, but that the astute Bavarian had deliberately taken or unwittingly absorbed quite a good deal from Gordon while he was a houseguest and was working in Boehm's shop. Today, however, Boehm is regarded as the creator of the flute as we know it.

As improvements were being made the flute lost much of its sweetness. The timbre became more reedy and powerful, and in the lower octave almost like a horn.

In 1838, a flute maker named Vincent Joseph Dorus, a Frenchman, further improved the flute with a new type of closed key, a G-sharp. In this same year, Auguste Buffet introduced a method of extending key action by use of a tubular rod axle. The axle joins a key that is operated by one of the playing fingers to a key that is out of the finger's reach. Buffet also invented the needle spring to activate keys more efficiently, and a D-sharp trill key. Other improvements continued to be made. In 1842, Cornelius Ward patented a flute that he claimed had greater mechanical ease than that of either Gordon or Boehm. In 1847, Boehm's flute changed back to the old cylindrical bore, which made the pitch more accurate and equalized the tone of the various registers.

There were some failures as flute makers tried to follow Boehm with their own improved models. Out of all the scramble, in 1849, came a very important addition to the flute —the B-flat lever, devised by an Italian, Giulio Briccialdi.

Commercial production of most of the famous early-day flutes was handled by an English firm, Rudall and Rose. This firm was established in 1821 by George Rudall, a flute professor, and John Mitchell Rose, a young flute maker of Edinburgh, Scotland. Other manufacturers at the time were Gerock and Wolfe; Godfrey and Lot; Thomas Prowse; and Boosey and Company, later to become famous in the music world as Boosey and Hawkes, and still thriving today.

No one musical instrument has ever had so many "inventors" as did the flute in the one hundred years preceding 1875. Many of these well-meaning improvers often worked their way up blind alleys, and many failed miserably. All together, they changed the simple pipe flute into a complicated and admirably sophisticated piece of musical mechanism.

More flute specimens survive than do those of any other wind instrument. If you would like to see some of the old-time flutes, visit the Library of Congress in Washington, D.C., where a marvelous assortment of antique flutes is on display in the Dayton C. Miller Collection. You will find rare and peculiar instruments—monuments to skill and determination. One instrument has a key used to trill C-sharp to D-sharp. Another can sound F-natural in three different ways. Most of them have a wild hodgepodge of keys and levers. All of them are interesting.

5. *The Making of a Flute*

Since 1847, when Theobald Boehm turned out an improved cylindrical model of the conical flute with which he had astounded flutists in 1832, there have been no vital changes in the instrument's structure. The tone holes on today's flute are in about the same positions as Boehm placed them. After much experimentation he determined where the holes should be in order to get the best intonation, with the tone even and of the right volume—and with the positions of the playing fingers taking secondary consideration. The mechanism today is essentially the same as in Boehm's flute; it involves the use of tubular axles, or sleeves, hinging on rod axles, which with stops, or clutches, and connecting pins, make possible the independent movement of the keys. The system of fingering is just as it was arranged by Boehm. The few minor changes since 1847 have been the adoption of needle springs on the keys; the moving of rod axles from the far to the near side of the tube; and the more widespread use of trill keys.

The materials for making flutes, however, are quite different today. At one time or another in the flute's history the instrument has been made of marble and jade, by the Greeks and Chinese; of terra-cotta and baked clay, by the Portuguese; of eagle and vulture bones, animal horn, porcelain, Dresden china, tortoiseshell inlaid in gold, papier-mâché, ivory, glass,

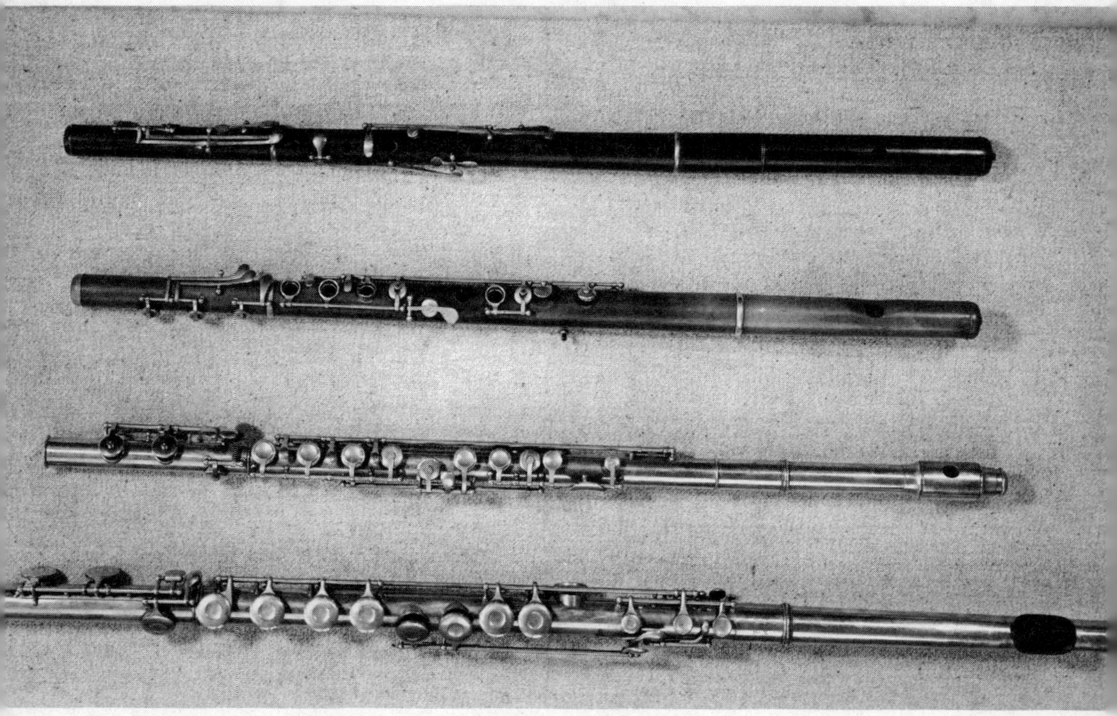

Four stages in the development of the Boehm system; reading from the top:

1829: A wooden flute with conical bore in style of Boehm's immediate predecessors.

c. 1832: Earliest known model of Boehm's improved system.

1848: Boehm's perfected model, made entirely of silver, with cylindrical bore.

After 1848: An alto flute with full Boehm mechanism.

wax—and even of leather, by an Edinburgh shoemaker in 1789. John Bunyan, the preacher who wrote *Pilgrim's Progress* when he was in jail, carved a flute from the leg of a prison chair. Walking-stick flutes, called *cannesflûtes*, were popular in France as late as 1880. Sometimes two such flutes were joined together to make a long staff on which duets could be played by two persons walking side by side. Some of the double *cannesflûtes* concealed a sword in the tube.

Many kinds of wood have been used for flutes: cocuswood, ebony, laurel, pine, and the South American granadilla. Fine flutes have been made of copper and platinum, and are still manufactured of gold. The most popular flute material today, however, is silver or silver-plated metal.

A flute's tone quality depends greatly upon the material of which the instrument's tube is made. Silver and gold produce tones of exquisite delicacy. Ebonite, the hard black vulcanized rubber used also for combs, makes a rich, mellow tone powerful enough to be heard over the other instruments of an orchestra.

The majority of modern flutes are made either in Boston, Massachusetts, or in Elkhart, Indiana, the musical-instrument capital of the United States. Two prominent Boston firms are the Wm. S. Haynes Company and the Verne Q. Powell Company (founded by an ex-Haynes employee and still bearing his name). Powell, a Kansas jeweler, was attracted to flute making in 1926 after he had heard a concert by Georges Barrère. Symphonic musicians consider the flutes of Haynes and Powell the finest made today. Four major flute manufacturers in Elkhart are Lynton, Selmer, Conn, and Gemeinhardt.

No flute manufacturer will reveal all his methods. Some of them are jealously guarded family secrets that are handed down from one generation to another.

It takes one man about three weeks of concentrated work to build a first-class custom-made flute. Most of the many parts are now machine-tooled, but some are still fashioned by hand with the same care and precision as that given to the making of fine watches and jewelry. A flute maker must be a man with patience and iron nerves. Measurements must be made to a hairbreadth, and everything fitted with scrupulous exactitude. Otherwise, the flute will not play well.

The key mechanism is in four separate sections; their assembly—by intricate soldering with noncorrosive solder and the use of tiny screws—calls for a steady hand and excellent eyes. Keys usually are drop-forged with the use of dies. Possibly the most precise job in assembling the key sections is fitting the padded keys to the tone holes. The keys must be seated absolutely right—loose enough so that they will respond to the player's touch, and tight enough so that not a particle of air can escape from around the edges when the keys are closed. This task takes experience. Most flute makers start working with the instrument when they are young men. They would not trade their craft for any other job. They fall in love with the flute after they have worked with it for awhile.

The older men bending over the workbenches in a flute factory have seen many changes in the craft. In the old days the tubing for flutes was cut from sheets, was rolled to the proper diameter, and was then sealed. Flute makers no longer bother with this laborious operation. Nowadays, flute tubing is seamless, and comes to the factory already made. The seamless tubes are formed from disks that are first struck into a cup shape by a large drop hammer and are then drawn over a steel mold core by a machine called a drawbench. On cheaper, or "commercial," models, the tone holes are made by a manufacturing process that draws them up out of the metal. The edges of the holes are then rolled smooth. The tone holes on professional flutes, however, are still cut, or punched, by hand.

Many independent individual flute makers are scattered about the country. Most of them are in business primarily to repair the larger woodwinds—those that have reed mouthpieces and are more fragile than the flute. Nothing much ever damages that instrument. Beyond getting out of adjustment or having a pad or a key wear out, it is fairly rugged. But every once in a while, something peculiar or spectacular does occur.

The most memorable flute catastrophe ever heard of happened in 1953 at the City Center of Music and Drama, a large auditorium formerly housing the New York City Opera and New York City Ballet, and now host theater to both resident and visiting dance and drama companies. During a ballet a well-known New York flutist, Fred Wilkins, happened to touch his silver flute both to his lighted metal music stand and to the iron railing that went around the orchestra pit. Somehow, the contact caused a short circuit. In a flash, the flute's keys, springs, and solder became a melted mess. The flute was put out of commission. Luckily, Wilkins was not burned, and a good flute maker was able to restore the instrument to perfect condition.

Flutes sometimes are trapped in fires or floods and have to be completely overhauled. Once, during a performance of the Ringling Bros. and Barnum & Bailey Circus at Madison Square Garden in New York, a runaway drill horse kicked a flute from the mouth of one of the bandsmen; it was not damaged much, but the flutist lost two teeth.

Backstage at the old Metropolitan Opera House, a flutist at rehearsal was once visiting a friend in the scenic department and accidentally dropped his instrument into a tub of paint. That flute had to be dismantled completely, and every part down to the smallest screw had to be wiped and cleaned.

The owners of these unfortunate flutes felt a sense of personal loss and injury, because the flute has such appeal for those who play it. After you have played the instrument for awhile, you will find that you too are fond of your flute.

6. *The Professional Flutist*

The life of a professional flutist is not nearly as glamorous as that of a concert pianist or violinist.

A flute player, no matter how exquisite his music, does not excite public imagination as a famous pianist or violinist does. If you eventually become a professional, your circle of admirers will be small, but it will be very, very genuine.

But first, be sure you really want a professional career as a flutist. It is not easy to face even a small audience, whether it be tolerant or critical. Serious concentration and control are needed to play the flute with other musicians, in an orchestra, with a small wind group, or even with only piano accompaniment.

To be a professional flutist requires lengthy training, which can run into a heavy financial investment. It may take some time to earn back the money spent on education. A beginning musician rarely earns much money.

Entrance standards are high for advanced musical education in a college or a conservatory. A student must take rigid examinations to prove how well he can handle his instrument. Often, even at high school level, there are tests for musical aptitude and proficiency.

Flutists remain generally unknown outside the profession, but music lovers are aware of many of the good ones. Severino

Georges Barrère.

Gazzelloni is considered to be one of the world's leading flute virtuosos today. Jean-Pierre Rampal is another famous flutist—one of the best. Also well known are Pierre Herichez, Maxence Larrieu, Alain Marion, Claude Monteux, and Michel Bebost—all Frenchmen, who traditionally are the finest wind instrumentalists. Some noteworthy flute players in the United States are Julius Baker, first flutist of the New York Philharmonic; Harold Bennett, formerly of the NBC Symphony Orchestra; James Politos, Metropolitan Opera first flutist; and Sebastian Caratelli, Radio City Music Hall Orchestra. Other outstanding present-day male flutists are Marcel Moyse and his son Louis; William Heil; Paige Brooks; and John Wummer.

Among noted female flutists of today are Elaine Shaffer, Paula Sylvester, Nancy Urrelman, and Doriot Dwyer, who is first flutist in the Boston Symphony Orchestra. Two master flutists of the recent past were William Kincaid of the Philadelphia Orchestra, and Georges Barrère, the celebrated first flutist with the New York Symphony Orchestra under Walter Damrosch. Contemporary flutists still recognize Barrère's superlative playing.

In jazz, as early as 1940, saxophonists began to double on the flute, but not until 1956 did the instrument rate a special category in the famous Readers' Popularity Poll of *Down Beat*, the jazz musicians' magazine.

Waymen Carver, in the Chick Webb band, played jazz flute on a couple of phonograph records in 1937; this was a pioneer attempt that no one took very seriously. A West Coast jazzman named Harry Klee did some flute work around 1944, but Frank Wellington, out of Kansas City, was the first jazz star to record successfully as a flute soloist.

Then, in 1953, Frank Wess, with the Count Basie band, and Clifford Everett (Bud) Shank, who was well known in West Coast jazz circles, began to use the flute often for solos and as a new voice in jazz ensembles. Around that same time, other jazz flute virtuosos appeared: Jerome Richardson, who also played jazz on the piccolo; Paul Horn, whose mother was pianist for Irving Berlin for years; Bobby Jasper, from Belgium; Jay Solomon (Herbie) Mann of Brooklyn, who has proven the most gifted of them all as a modernist on the flute. Another remarkable jazz flutist of today is Yusef Lateef (real name, William Evans), an ex-member of the Dizzy Gillespie band. Flutes appear quite often with rock and folk-rock groups.

During the instrument's early days there were many more

Louis Hotteterre, from the frontispiece of his instruction manual, Principles of the Transverse or German Flute.

flute virtuosos than there are today. In those times the flute was much more in evidence and flutists were highly regarded public figures.

A Frenchman named Philbert was one of the first virtuosos of the one-keyed flute—an instrument popular for over one hundred years, from 1660 to 1768. Philbert, a great favorite of Louis XIV, sang for the king's courtiers and acted as a mimic besides playing the flute. He was not, however, a professional court jester.

Several excellent flutists of concert caliber were members of the Hotteterre family of flute makers in the late 1660's. The most renowned was Louis Hotteterre, who in 1697 played the first transverse flute to appear in the Paris Opera. The most accomplished player, though the least known, of the Hotteterres was Louis' cousin Jacques.

Jean Baptiste Loeillet was the first man to play the German flute in England. Upon his arrival there in 1705, he was made principal flutist in London's first operatic orchestra, at the Queen's Theatre in the section of the city called Haymarket. Loeillet became one of the most sought-after flute teachers of the day.

The finest flute player in Germany at that time was August Schroeck, noted for his correct intonation and superb clear tone. He was a chamber musician at the Prussian court and first flutist at the Royal Opera in Berlin.

Pierre Gabriel Buffardin, born in France in the latter part of the seventeenth century, was noted for his neatness and rapidity of execution in playing the flute.

One of Buffardin's pupils was Johann Joachim Quantz (1697–1773), who became possibly the most distinguished flutist of his day. As an orphaned child, Quantz was adopted by an uncle, who was a court musician and tailor. When his

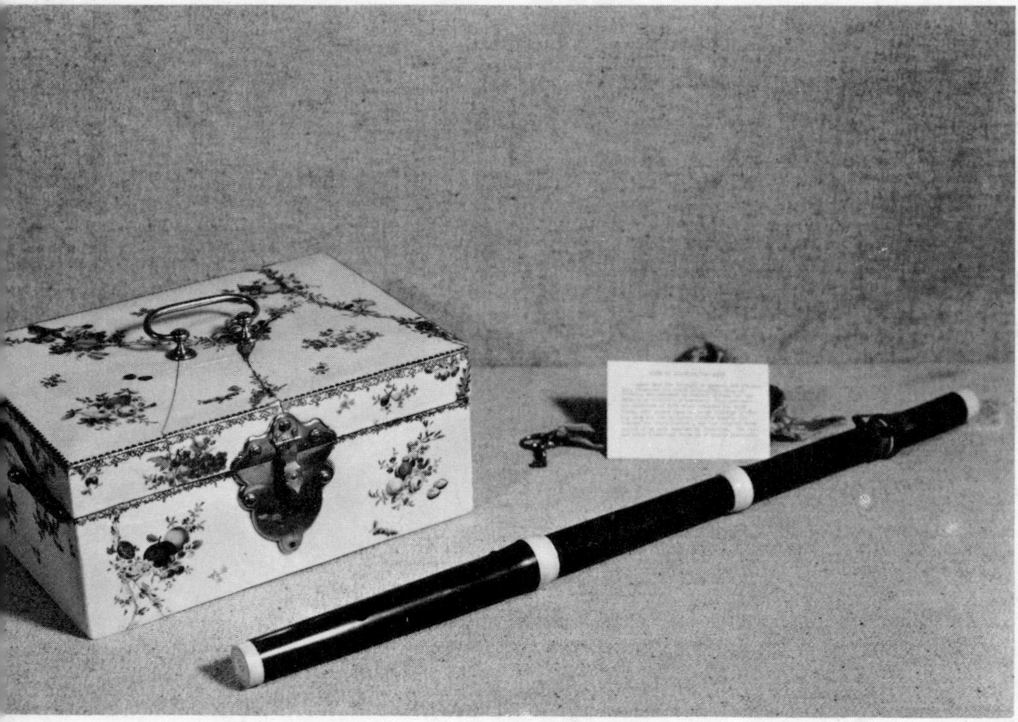

Flute made for Frederick the Great by Johann Joachim Quantz. Background: flute case of Berlin porcelain.

uncle died, young Quantz was taken in hand by another court musician and soon was able to play a good many musical instruments: violin, trumpet, violoncello, viola da gamba, harpsichord, and hautboy, or oboe. After a great deal of experimenting as a musician he finally took up the flute in 1718.

Under the patronage of the king of Poland, Quantz's rise as a flutist was rapid. He soon became flute teacher, secretly, to the young crown prince of Prussia, who had been forbidden to play the instrument by his father, Frederick Wilhelm. The queen of Prussia, in defiance of her husband, furnished money for lessons. Quantz frequently had to hide in a woodbox in the prince's quarters to avoid the wrath of the king, who had threatened beheading to anyone who dared teach his son such a disgusting, dreadful instrument.

When young Frederick, who came to be known as Frederick the Great, inherited the throne in 1740, Quantz was made court composer and the new king's flute teacher for life. The salary was high for those days. Quantz's duties were to play in the court orchestra; to attend the king daily; to play duets with him; to try out new concertos composed by the king; and to beat time to flute music played by His Majesty in nightly concerts held in the palace. In spite of such a rigorous schedule, Quantz lived to be seventy-seven years old.

Frederick was a very active flutist, if not a particularly good one. He composed hundreds of flute solos and concertos. His accompanist on the harpsichord was Carl Philipp Emanuel Bach, a son of Johann Sebastian Bach. His Majesty thought so highly of his own ability on the flute that once, after performing one of his own compositions rather poorly, he exclaimed in delight and self-admiration, "What rhythm!" To this, long-suffering young Bach muttered crustily, "What rhythms!"

According to Quantz, one of the truly great flute virtuosos of his time was Michel Blavet, who played left-handed.

Another accomplished player, Felix Rault, born in 1736, was a protégé of the great Blavet.

A little later, an eminent flutist was Jean Louis Tulou, born in 1786 and at fifteen regarded as the finest flute player in France. At eighteen, he was appointed the principal flutist at the Italian Opera; at twenty-seven, he held the top flute position at the Grand Opera in Paris.

Once, when a joint of Tulou's wooden flute split from end

"A Concert of Frederick the Great"; a re-creation by the German artist Adolph Menzel.

Louis Drouet.

to end, he mended it onstage with some thread and a piece of wax, then continued with his solo. He executed it so brilliantly that, at its end, the audience rose, and cheered and applauded for thirteen minutes.

Tulou was a great rival of Louis Drouet, born in 1792, the youngest professional flute player of all time, who began playing in public at the age of four. At eighteen, Drouet was appointed flute soloist to the king of Holland. Young Drouet played on a flute of glass, which had keys set with precious stones.

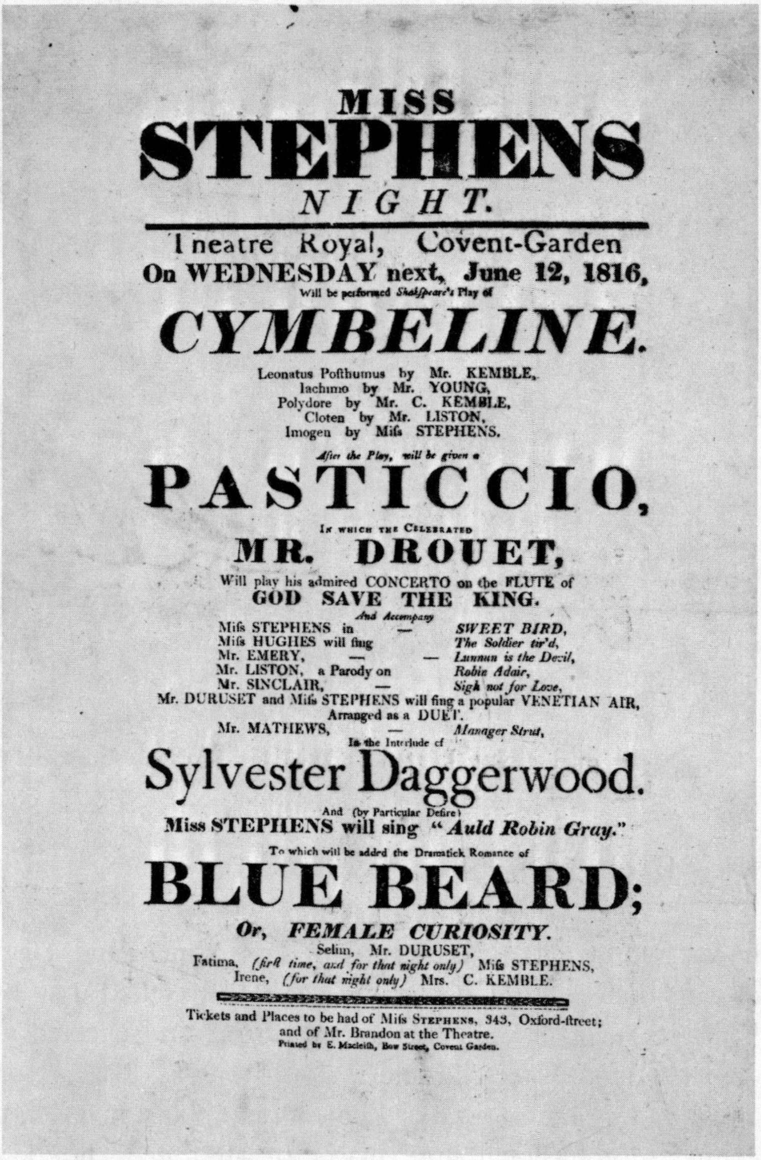

A theater bill featuring Louis Drouet in the early nineteenth century.

A one-keyed flute, made in nine sections by Heinrich Grenser of Dresden, late eighteenth century.

Other historic youthful flutists were Benjamin Hallet, who made his debut at the Drury Lane Theatre in London at the age of five, and Karl Grenser, who faced the public with his flute when he was only six.

Perhaps the greatest of early flute players was Charles Nicholson, born in 1795 in Liverpool. Nicholson loved to

Charles Nicholson.

play *cadenzas*, brilliant passages at the end of the first section of a concerto, which were almost as long as the whole concerto. His cadenzas usually were followed by a trill, then called a shake, of fabulous length. Nicholson was much admired for his purity of intonation, his perfection of double tonguing, and the rich contrast and variety in his playing. He was famous for a whirlwind rush of notes from the top of his instrument to the bottom; he had an especially beautiful kind of vibration and a trick of gliding that no one else seemed able to master.

A pupil of Nicholson's, Joseph Richardson, born in 1814, became the most popular flute soloist of England. He was prominent as the chief attraction at the promenade concerts that were part of the London social scene in the early part of the nineteenth century. Richardson had perfect control over the mechanism of his flute.

An astonishing one-armed virtuoso of the flute in the 1840's was Count Rebsomen. His instrument was fixed to a vertical support clamped to a tabletop. The left-hand fingering was done by the second joints of the right hand's fingers on holes placed between those normally used by that hand.

Count Rebsomen, the one-armed virtuoso of the flute.

Important flute players of the later nineteenth century were John Summers Cox, featured with John Philip Sousa's band, and Otto Oesterle, for many years first flutist with the New York Philharmonic Orchestra. Two others who should be mentioned are Siegfried Orgelist, who at the age of thirteen was principal flutist of the Carlsbad Symphony Orchestra and as a very young man joined the London Symphony Orchestra under Sir Thomas Beecham; and Robert Sidney Pratten, a child prodigy, who as an adult virtuoso was known for his powerful tone, easily heard over the loudest tones of an orchestra's brass section.

The majority of flute players today are content to be amateurs, playing their instruments only for pleasure. There have been some distinguished amateur flute players. Among them have been George Washington, Jean Jacques Rousseau, Henry David Thoreau, Robert Louis Stevenson, Lord Byron, Leonardo da Vinci, Benvenuto Cellini, and Henry VIII, who favored the recorder, or vertical flute. Other royal flutists have been Francis I of Austria and England's Henry V, Henry VI, and George II.

An amateur flutist probably has more fun with his instrument than does a professional. But whether you turn professional or remain an amateur, by taking up the flute you have become a member of a select group playing one of the loveliest musical instruments ever created.

7. *Flute Music and Its Composers*

The best way to understand music is to listen to it a great deal, either live or on recordings.

Music does not always communicate itself easily. To appreciate a piece of music, you must give it serious attention. Being able to recognize and evaluate the technical qualities of the music will help you to comprehend what the composer and the performer are expressing through their art.

When you listen to music, whether it be flute or any other kind, try to feel what the composer had in mind. Does he mean to be funny or sad? Hopeful or despairing? Is he speaking sweetly or sourly? Harshly or gently? Is he expressing strength, weakness, cruelty, or compassion? What is in his thoughts? Love, tenderness, mysticism, grandeur, despair, revolution, piety, fury? All these abstractions and many others can be expressed by music.

You will appreciate flute music more if you know something about the structure of music in general. Musical tone has *pitch* (highness or lowness), *duration* (longness or shortness), *intensity* (softness or loudness), and *timbre*, or tone color. Different composers make different uses of musical tone.

Musicians compose their works by arranging notes or tones in patterns of time. Music depends on *rhythm*, which is the regular beat—the pattern of music's flow or movement. Without rhythm, there would be little meaning, strength, or life in *melody,* which is a parade of varying notes following one another and having a relationship to each other and to the whole. Rhythm can exist without melody—for instance, the simple beating of a single drum is rhythmic, but it may not be melodic.

When two or more individual and independent melodies are fitted together to be played at the same time to make a satisfying musical whole, the result is called *counterpoint,* or *polyphony* (from the Greek *poly,* meaning "many," and *phonos,* meaning "sound," or "voices").

When you are listening to any musical composition, feel the *tempo,* the rate of speed at which the rhythm is played. Tempo is marked on a musical score by these terms from the Italian: *adagio,* meaning "slow"; *andante,* meaning "moderate pace"; *allegro,* meaning "fast"; *vivace,* meaning "lively and faster"; *presto,* meaning "very fast"; and *prestissimo,* meaning "as fast as can be performed."

Pay attention to the *harmony,* which is the way chords are arranged. Simple harmony is mostly in four parts: treble, alto, tenor, and bass. Chords are tone patterns made by playing at the same time three or more notes of different pitch. There are consonant chords, made up of notes at certain intervals; they are satisfying and restful. There are dissonant chords, made up of notes at certain other intervals; they sound restless and incomplete. The way in which chords follow each other and move along in tone patterns has been governed by certain customary rules, which composers often choose to violate. Know the rules, and listen to learn how they have been sidestepped.

All music is written to some form. Other words for "form"

are "structure" and "design." Each musical piece has its own master plan for holding together rhythm, melody, tempo, and harmony. In all forms, patterns of rhythm, melody, and harmony repeat and contrast with one another to make an interesting musical unity.

The form may involve many instruments, as in a symphony, and it may be in combination with human voices, as in an opera, an oratorio, or a musical comedy. Or the form may be for one instrument or a small group of instruments, as in a sonata. The form may be adapted to combinations of solo instruments, such as duets, trios, quartets, quintets, sextets, septets, octets, and nonets—which are groups of two, three, four, five, six, seven, eight, and nine instruments, respectively. The form may also be a concerto, a large-scale composition in which a solo performer and an orchestra play together.

Usually a concerto has three movements. Traditionally the first movement is fast, closing with a brilliant display solo called a *cadenza*—formerly sometimes written by the soloist himself, or made up by him on the spot, but now more often written by the composer. A concerto's second movement is slow and lyrical, often in song form. The closing movement is lively, mostly in *rondo* style—that is, with sections that repeat themselves between contrasting sections.

As a solo instrument, the flute performs most often in the concerto and sonata forms. Flutes also play together in small woodwind groups or in a symphony, which is generally in four movements.

The first two movements of a symphony are generally the same as for the concerto—but without the cadenza. The symphony's third movement is often either a *minuet* or a *scherzo* (Italian for "joke"), a fast-paced, humorous piece of music.

The *finale*, or ending movement, is customarily either a theme and variations or a rondo.

A first-class symphony orchestra usually has four flutes in its woodwind section, which includes also four clarinets, three oboes, four bassoons, and one English horn.

You will get more enjoyment from a flute recital or a symphonic concert in which flutes play a part if you have some understanding of how the composer put his music together to get the results he was seeking. But remember that music is not meant primarily to exercise the intellect. Music is mostly aimed at the emotions and the senses. Feel it in your heart.

Each composer for the flute has written for this instrument in his own personal style and may also have been reflecting the period in which he lived. Try to catch the quirks of the composer's personality and the mood of his time.

Most early flutists were also composers for the instrument. In the late seventeenth century, Louis Hotteterre produced six major works. The next composer of note to follow him was Jean Baptiste Loeillet, also a master of the one-keyed flute. He wrote many sonatas for the instrument.

In the early eighteenth century came Johann Joachim Quantz. He became a prolific composer. While he worked as flute tutor to Frederick the Great, Quantz turned out 300 concertos; 200 solo sonatas; 26 sonatas for flute and harpsichord; duets too numerous to count; 39 trios, mostly for two flutes with bass; and a horde of studies, caprices, preludes, and practice pieces for the flute. The left-handed Michel Blavet was also an excellent flutist-composer of that time.

In the late seventeenth and early eighteenth centuries, both Johann Sebastian Bach (1685–1750) and George Frideric Handel (1685–1759) wrote for the simple, one-keyed flute.

Other composers of the time who wrote for the flute included Bach's good friend, Georg Philipp Telemann (1681–1767), and their great Italian contemporary, Antonio Vivaldi (1678–1741). Both Bach's eldest son, Carl Philipp Emanuel (1714–1788), and his youngest son, Johann Christian (1735–1782), also contributed notably to flute literature.

The flute of Bach's day was rudimentary, compared to the instrument played today. In many of Bach's scores the word *flauto,* for flute, meant the recorder; *flauto piccolo* indicated the use of the French *flageolet,* and not a transverse piccolo. Bach's compositions for the flute show disregard for the wind player's need to breathe or rest his lips. Bach believed that a worthwhile musician should be able to conquer his instrument and get from it everything he possibly could. Bach's understanding of the emotional range of the flute was unique in his time.

Bach wrote many works that had parts for the flute. Among them were three sonatas for unaccompanied flute, three sonatas for accompanied flute, and a sonata for flute, violin, and a keyboard instrument. (Since the piano was in its infancy in Bach's day, keyboard accompaniments were written for earlier instruments, such as the harpsichord.)

One of the loveliest works dating from this time, and perhaps the finest of Bach's compositions for flute, is his Sonata in B Minor; its first movement is one of his supreme creations. Bach's Sonata in A Minor is memorable in that the opening theme combines with new subjects in all four sections of the sonata without losing its identity. The *finale* of the Sonata in E Minor is a fascinating example of Bach's rejection of formal techniques.

In addition, there are many important flute passages in Bach's larger works, including his oratorios and *concerti grossi*

Johann Sebastian Bach.

Georg Philipp Telemann.

Wolfgang Amadeus Mozart.

Franz Joseph Haydn.

(concertos in which a small group of instrumentalists is pitted against an orchestra).

Among other works employing the flute, Handel wrote various solos, sonatas for flute with accompaniment, and three songs ("Sweet Bird That Shun'st," "Softest Sounds," and "In Gentle Murmurs").

The two composers who dominated the later eighteenth century were Franz Joseph Haydn (1732–1809) and Wolfgang Amadeus Mozart (1756–1791).

Haydn's compositions for flute are three trios for flutes and violoncello, and a sonata for flute and pianoforte.

Mozart wrote many works that had parts for the flute. Among them were two concertos for flute; one for flute and harp; a *Grand Duo* (duet) for flute and pianoforte; three quartets for flute and strings; a quintet for flute, two violins, viola, and violoncello; a sextet for violin, flute, viola, violoncello, and two horns; a rondo for flute and pianoforte; and an *Andante* for flute and orchestra. But perhaps the most famous flute passages ever written by Mozart were those he wrote for his last opera, *The Magic Flute*.

A contemporary of Mozart's, and a much more prolific composer for the flute, was Franz Anton Hoffmeister (1754–1812). He wrote 24 concertos, 6 quintets, 9 quartets, 9 trios, 21 duets, and 50 cadenzas.

The four-keyed flute came into being in the last quarter of the eighteenth century—some say as early as 1774. Early-nineteenth-century flute makers offered instruments with as many as eight keys.

For the flute with four keys and more, Ludwig van Beethoven created some hauntingly beautiful music. He wrote a great deal of flute chamber music; thirty-two variations for flute and piano, and six *Varied Themes* for those two instruments. He also composed a duet for two flutes; a quintet for piano and winds; and a septet for strings and winds—along with two serenades (for flute and piano, and for flute, violin, and viola) and a sonata for flute and piano.

Beethoven also used the flute to achieve special effects in his larger works: In the second movement of his *Symphony No. 6* (*"The Pastoral"*), for example, the flutes imitate the sound of birds in the forest.

Lesser-known flute composers by the score crowded the early part of the nineteenth century. A giant among them was Tranquille Benoit-Berbiguier, born in 1782, who started out to be a lawyer, but was captured by the flute. He composed thirteen concertos, many pieces for flute with piano or violin, and innumerable works for two and three flutes. He played left-handed, and one tricky piece was written for a friend who had only one arm.

Rafael Dressler stands out, with more than one hundred flute compositions. There was also Friedrich Kuhlau, born in a village in Hanover in 1786. Although Kuhlau, as a youth, had lost one eye when he fell in the dark while carrying water from a well, he became first flutist with the Royal Band and Opera of Copenhagen, Denmark. There he composed over one hundred concertos and scores of other flute works; over two hundred of his compositions have been preserved. Kuhlau, called the Beethoven of the flute, did more to raise the standards of flute music than any other composer of his time.

Jean Louis Tulou, Johann Wilhelm Gabrielski, and Anton Bernhard Fuerstenau also turned out great stacks of flute music. The flute concertos of Louis Drouet were very popular. Eugene Walckier composed distinctive flute chamber music, including quartets for flute and other wind instruments. Kaspar Kummer was another distinguished flute composer of the

Franz Anton Hoffmeister.

Tranquille Benoit-Berbiguier.

Rafael Dressler.

Peter
Ilyitch
Tchaikovsky.

Felix
Mendelssohn.

Hector
Berlioz.

same period; his list of works is lengthy. Any listing of early-nineteenth-century flute composers would be incomplete without the names of Heinrich Soussmann, Paul Hippolyte Camus, José Maria del Carmen Ribas, Robert Frisch, Giulio Briccialdi, and Robert Sidney Pratten.

Music masters of the early- and mid-nineteenth century relied heavily on the flute for unusual effects in their orchestral compositions. Franz Schubert gave a great deal of solo work to flutes. The flute stands out in Felix Mendelssohn's *St. Paul* Oratorio and in his *Midsummer Night's Dream* music. Rossini's *William Tell* Overture would not be nearly so effective without its flutes.

In his opera *The Flying Dutchman*, Richard Wagner used flutes to create a storm musically. Flutes also have major roles in Wagner's *Die Walküre*, *Siegfried*, and *Tannhäuser*.

Hector Berlioz, who himself was a flutist, was fond of combining the flute with a harp.

Anton Dvořák's Third Rhapsody and his Second, Fourth, and Fifth Symphonies have wonderful flute solos. In his *Spectre's Bride*, Dvořák uses the flute for the cockcrow at sunrise, and a rapid diatonic run on the flute from low G to middle G indicates the hero leaping a wall.

Edvard Grieg made great use of the flute in his *Peer Gynt* suites; and the soldiers' march in Act I of Georges Bizet's *Carmen* is played by flutes initially, before the full orchestra takes up the melody.

Peter Ilyitch Tchaikovsky, who as a young man played the flute professionally, made excellent use of the instrument in many of his works. He was often criticized for making flute parts too difficult. His Suite for Orchestra, No. 1, for instance, has three flutes playing triplets for twenty-two bars without a break for breathing.

It is likely that the most beautiful passages for flute in all of orchestral literature occur in Claude Debussy's *Prélude à l'Après-midi d'un Faune* (*Prelude to the Afternoon of a Faun*), first performed in 1894.

A great deal of music for the flute has been written in more recent times. Three especially lovely modern-day flute compositions are the *Partita for Flute, Oboe, String Quartet, and Harpsichord,* by Vittorio Rieti, composed in an eighteenth-century vein; the *Concerto Antoniano,* for flute and orchestra; and *Burlesca,* a duet for flute and guitar. The latter two pieces are by Nicholas Flagello, brother of a famous Metropolitan Opera singer.

As you can see, you will never lack pieces to play on your flute.

Perhaps someday you will be able to sit down and write some flute music yourself. Several young contemporary musicians have composed interesting offbeat pieces for the recorder, the vertical fipple flute. There is Stephen Hartke's *I Got Them Perth Amboy Blues and Vermilions,* for recorders and harpsichord; E. J. Miller's *Song,* for unaccompanied alto recorder; and H. U. Staep's *Dialogue,* for recorders and harpsichord. Look them up. You are sure to find them intriguing. And ask at your local music store for jazz and folk music for the flute. There is quite a lot of it around.

8. The Care of Your Flute

Just because a flute is small and convenient to handle does not mean that it needs less care than a larger instrument. Any musical instrument must be conscientiously looked after or it will not give its best performance.

When your flute is not in use, keep it in its padded case, with the lid closed and latched. Do not store it in a high place from which it may fall, with damaging effects. Do not place it where someone can sit on it or stumble over it. Be careful not to strike anything with your flute. A hard bump can cause its delicate mechanism to get out of adjustment.

Handle your flute carefully. To avoid injury to its mechanism, the middle section should always be grasped by its upper end and never in the middle or at the lower end where the keys are. Similarly, the foot joint should be handled at its lower end. Do not force the sections together or pull them apart roughly; be gentle about it. Grease or any other lubricant should not be used to make flute joints slide more easily. Instead, to keep the joints from sticking, wipe them carefully inside and out with a small damp cloth, and then polish them with a dry one.

Keep the flute keys reasonably clean. After each playing, wipe your flute with a damp cloth and polish it with a dry one. Make this a habit, for it is important in preventing the tarnishing of silver instruments and the corrosion of plated ones. Marks made by sweaty fingers can mar the surface of your instrument by oxidation. Unless you remove the sweaty marks, rough spots on the smooth surface of your flute will develop within a few weeks. In wiping and polishing, be careful not to snag the cloth on the keys. Do not apply pressure to them, for this may accidentally bend them.

Do not let dust collect inside the flute's tube. To keep it whistle-clean, pull or push a soft silk scarf through it every once in a while.

A frequent change of the flute's oil is a splendid idea. Over a period of time, oil on the moving parts of a flute has a tendency to gum up and become sticky and thick from dust, so hindering the easy movement of the keys. Your flute's mechanism can be kept in first-class condition by wiping the moving parts clean and reoiling them about once or twice a year. Use a special oil that you can get from your local music store. Or use jeweler's watch oil instead; this, too, is usually available at a music store.

Be careful not to get oil on the pads, as this will cause them to dry out and so will keep them from closing the holes properly. Never let the pads get wet.

Do not use silver polish on your flute, for it might gum up the pivot screws and damage the pads. If your flute really needs polishing, give this job to a trusted repairman. You should take your flute to him anyway for an annual checkup. Every three years your instrument should have a complete overhauling. It takes an expert's practiced eye to spot incipient defects that in time will affect your playing. The metal of the keys and levers is subject to wear from the countless number of times they move. An injured pad may need to be replaced; or a spring may have lost its springiness or be ready to break.

Last, but not least, write out a small card with your name, address, and phone number, and paste it inside the lid of the carrying case, so that if you forget and leave it somewhere, the flute can be returned to you easily.

Finale

One of the greatest rewards you will get from flute playing will be the satisfaction of having mastered this rather difficult member of the woodwind family.

All the tedious practicing, the finger aches, the stretchings of your mouth muscles, will be forgotten once you have learned to make your flute sing the way it is meant to. After you have overcome the technical problems yourself, you will more fully appreciate the artistry that a professional flutist puts into his playing. You will be astonished at how much a flute or symphony concert will mean to you and how much pleasure it will bring to you.

You may want to read more about the flute, and study the lives of famous players of this glorious instrument, or learn more about the composers for it, both past and present. That can be a pleasant pastime or an absorbing hobby for you.

Keep scrapbooks on any flute artists you hear in concerts. Save their programs so that you will better remember those joyous occasions.

Buy records made by flute virtuosos. Listen to them carefully so that you will understand more about the instrument you have chosen to play. Try to get records of the pieces you are studying, so that you can compare your playing with that of a professional. You will surely find that your interpretation differs. You may discover that in some passages you are more faithful to the music as it is written.

As a flute player and musician, you will find that your outlook on life has changed. A flutist is always welcome in any musical gathering; he is well respected, for musicians know that playing the flute well is a real accomplishment. You will make new friends who like to talk about some of the subjects in which you are interested; these discussions will start you thinking about the direction in which you are heading.

As a music player rather than a mere spectator, you may want to join your school orchestra or band. There you will learn the joy of being a disciplined member of a musical team.

With friends who play wind instruments, you might form a small ensemble. Through such group music-making you will all learn tolerance and something of give-and-take fellowship. You might become good enough to get paying engagements at local clubs, meetings, dinners, and parties. Arrange simple musical afternoons or evenings to benefit some useful social service or charity.

Perhaps you will be able to go to a summer music camp. These camps are at the seashore, in lake country, and in the mountains. Young people there study music with professionals, play their own instruments, and perform in concerts with students of their own age level and proficiency, while enjoying such outdoor recreational activities as swimming, hiking, cookouts, horseback riding, tennis, volleyball, and other court games.

A book called *A Parent's Guide to Music Lessons*, by Wills and Manners (Harper & Row), carries a handy listing of more than two hundred music camps located in forty-six states. Many of them are in California, Texas, and Illinois, but there is even one in Alaska. Up-to-date listings of music camps can be had from the Association of Private Camps, 55 West 42nd Street, New York, N.Y., or the American Camping Association, 342 Madison Avenue, New York, N.Y. For camps abroad sponsored by the International Federation of Music Youth, write to Jeunesses Musicales, Palais des Beaux Arts, Rue Baron Horte, Brussels, Belgium; or to Jeunesses Musicales du Canada, 430 St. Josephs Oueste, Montreal, Canada. For other music camps in Canada, write to the Canadian Culture Information Centre, 56 Sparks Street, Ottawa, Canada.

Be sure you apply early for admission to a music camp, as the positions for flutists fill up soon. Always more flute players apply than can be accommodated.

Although there are many openings for flutists in the ranks of professional musicians, you may not wish to make a career of flute playing. Whether you do, or whether you play just for pleasure, you and your flute will certainly add beauty to the world around you. Flute music can brighten the drabbest places and the darkest thoughts. Stay with your flute through thick and thin. It will be a friend always.

Glossary

ADAGIO—Slow, an indication of tempo, used as a direction in music.

AIR REED—A flat stream of air made by compressing the lips; the air blown by a flute player across the embouchure.

ALLEGRO—Fast, lively, an indication of tempo, used as a direction in music.

ALTO FLUTE—A flute on which the lowest note is a G, instead of a C as in the regular concert flute pitched one fourth higher than the alto.

AMPLITUDE—The loudness of a sound.

ANDANTE—Going, moving, not as slow as *adagio*, an indication of tempo, used as a direction in music.

ARPEGGIO—Notes of a chord played rapidly, one after the other, ripplingly, instead of all at the same time.

BASS FLUTE—A flute pitched one full octave below the C flute.

BASSOON—A large woodwind instrument with a reedy tone, played by blowing against a double reed in a curved tubular mouthpiece of metal.

BEAKED FLUTE—A whistle flute, the recorder, called beaked because of the shape of its mouthpiece.

BODY—The middle section of a flute's tube.

BORE—The interior diameter of the flute.

CADENZA—In a concerto, a brilliant unaccompanied solo section, formerly improvised, now more often written by the composer.

CAPRICE—A whimsical musical work in free, irregular form; also called *capriccio.*

CHORD—A tone pattern made by playing three or more notes at the same time.

CHROMATIC—Progressing by half tones.

CLARINET—A tubular, keyed woodwind instrument with a bell end; it is played by blowing against a flat reed clamped to the mouthpiece.

CLOSED KEY—In wind instruments, a key which has been sprung to uncover a tone hole.

CONCERTO—A large-scale musical composition, putting together an orchestra and one or more solo instruments.

COUNTERPOINT—Two or more melodies played together at the same time to achieve a definite harmonic effect. (Also called Polyphony.)

CRESCENDO—Growing, an increase in the loudness of music (used as a musical direction).

CROSS-FINGERING—Creating a point of no vibration on a woodwind instrument by covering a tone hole below the one that is sounding; fingering out of serial order in the playing of certain wind instruments.

DIMINUENDO—Diminishing; decreasing in loudness (used as a direction in music).

DOUBLE BASSOON—A large bassoon pitched an octave lower than the bassoon.

DUET—A musical composition for two instruments or two voices.

EBONITE—A hard vulcanized rubber sometimes used in making woodwind instruments.

EMBOUCHURE—The mouth hole cut into the side of a flute's tube, against which a player blows to make a tone. Also, the muscular position of the player's mouth.

ENGLISH HORN—A woodwind instrument similar to the oboe, with a bulb-shaped bell end, and pitched a fifth lower than the oboe.

FIFE—A woodwind instrument pitched between the concert flute and the piccolo.

FINGER HOLES—The holes in a woodwind's tube, uncovered by the fingers or keys to make the different notes; also called tone holes.

FIPPLE—The slotted plug mouthpiece of a recorder.

FLAGEOLET—A small-sized recorder.

FLUTE-À-BEC—A beaked recorder.

FOOT JOINT—The open-end section of a flute; the end farthest from the mouthpiece end.

FORM—Structure, or the design or master plan, of a piece of music.

FORTISSIMO—Very loud, an indication used as a playing direction in music.

HARMONICS—Overtones, or higher tones that faintly accompany the fundamental tone produced by a musical instrument; in a woodwind instrument they are created by the vibration of small sections of the air column.

HARMONY—The way tones and chords are arranged in relation to one another in a piece of music.

HARPSICHORD—A plucked-string keyboard musical instrument.

HEAD—The closed-end or mouthpiece end of a flute's tube.

KEY—In woodwinds, an arrangement of levers and pads used to open and close a tone hole, or finger hole.

LEGATO—A smooth, connected manner of playing musical notes (often used as a direction in music).

Melody—A parade of notes, one following the other meaningfully, and all having a relationship one to another.

Minuet—A slow, stately seventeenth-century French dance for groups of couples; written in triple time.

Needle spring—A spring of steel wire used on a flute key.

Nonet—A musical composition for nine instruments or nine voices.

Nose flute—A flute blown through a nostril rather than by mouth.

Oboe—A woodwind instrument played with a double-reed mouthpiece and having a high, penetrating, melancholy tone.

Ocarina—An Italian globular flute usually made of clay or porcelain.

Octave—A succession of eight notes comprising a scale, the eighth one having twice as many vibrations per second as the first.

Octet—A musical composition for eight instruments or eight voices.

Open key—In wind instruments, a key that is sprung to close a tone hole.

Overblowing—Blowing an airstream of more intensity and compression on a wind instrument to play higher notes in the overtone series.

Panpipes—A row of tubes, graduated in length and bound together, with the mouthpieces in an even row. Played by blowing across the open mouthpiece ends; also called syrinx.

Piccolo—A small flute, minus the foot joint that gives the flute its three lowest keys.

Pitch—The relative highness or lowness of a musical tone.

Polyphony—See Counterpoint.

PRELUDE—An introductory section or movement in a piece of music.

PRESTISSIMO—As fast as a player can go, an indication of tempo, used as a musical direction.

PRESTO—Very fast, an indication of tempo, used as a musical direction.

QUARTET—A musical composition for four instruments or four voices.

QUINTET—A musical composition for five instruments or five voices.

RECORDER—A straight flute (played vertically) equipped with a beak mouthpiece.

REED—A flexible blade, usually a piece of cane, held fast at one end and placed in the mouthpiece of a reed woodwind (clarinet, oboe, bassoon, saxophone) so that it vibrates when a column of air is blown against it.

RHYTHM—The forward-moving organization of music in respect to time; the regular occurrence of beat.

RING KEY—A springing metal ring suspended over an open hole and connected with a lever to another key over a helping hole that is beyond reach of the player's fingers. The helping key stays open and functions as a correction as long as the hole under the ring key is open.

RONDO—A form of instrumental music in which the principal theme repeats in the same key, with contrasting themes or sections in between.

SAXOPHONE—A large, keyed reed woodwind with a curved head joint and a large bell-shaped end, invented in 1854 by Adolphe Sax; made of brass, and resembling a bass clarinet.

SCALE—A series of tones within an octave which are used as the basis of musical composition.

SCHERZO—Italian for "joke"; a light, fast-paced, whimsical short piece of music.

SEMITONE—The twelfth part of an octave, the smallest normal interval in modern music of the Western world.

SEPTET—A musical composition for seven instruments or seven voices.

SERENADE—A musical composition suitable for performance outdoors at night; it is generally light and entertaining.

SEXTET—A musical composition for six instruments or six voices.

SHAKE—On wind instruments, a trill, or rapid alternation of two musical notes.

SOLFEGGI—Practice pieces.

SOLO—A musical composition for only one instrument or one voice.

SONATA—A composition performed as a solo or as a piece for piano and another instrument. It has three or more movements.

STACCATO—Notes held as briefly as possible, and detached from one another (often used as a direction in music).

SYMPHONY—A work for orchestra, in four movements. Because it often has much the same form as the sonata, it is often called a "sonata for orchestra."

SYRINX—See Panpipes.

TEMPO—The rate of speed of a musical composition.

TIMBRE—The quality of musical tone: thin, thick, light, dark, etc. Also called tone color.

TONE COLOR—See Timbre.

TONE HOLES—See Finger holes.

TRANSVERSE FLUTE—A flute played in a horizontal position.

TRILL—In wind instruments, a rapid alternation of two musical notes.

Trill key—In woodwinds, the key that is used to make a trill.

Trio—A musical composition for three instruments or three voices.

Triplet—A group of three notes performed in the time of two of the same value.

Vivace—Lively, an indication of tempo, used as a direction in music.

Whistle—An instrument on which whistling sounds can be made by blowing through a mouthpiece into a cavity or against the edge of a hole.

Suggested Books for Reading and Reference

Flutes and Flutists

√BAINES, ANTHONY. *Woodwind Instruments and Their History.* Rev. ed. New York: W. W. Norton & Company, 1963.

BOEHM, THEOBALD. *The Flute and Flute Playing.* Gloucester, Mass.: Peter Smith.

CARSE, ADAM. *Musical Wind Instruments.* 2nd ed. New York: Da Capo Press, 1965.

Musical Background

BERNSTEIN, LEONARD. *The Infinite Variety of Music.* New York: Simon & Schuster, 1966.

COPLAND, AARON. *Copland on Music.* New York: W. W. Norton & Company, 1963.

√FEATHER, LEONARD. *The Book of Jazz.* Rev. ed. New York: Horizon Press, 1965.

GOLDRON, ROMAIN. *Minstrels and Masters.* (Music of History Series, vol. 3.) Garden City, N.Y.: Doubleday & Company, 1968.

———. *Music of the Renaissance.* (Music of History Series, vol. 4.) Garden City, N.Y.: Doubleday & Company, 1968.

McKinney, Howard D., & Anderson, W. R. *Discovering Music.* 4th ed. New York: American Book Company, 1952.

Moore, Douglas. *Listening to Music.* New York: W. W. Norton & Company, 1963.

Seligmann, Jean, and Danziger, Juliet. *The Meaning of Music: The Young Concertgoer's Guide.* New York: World Publishing Company, 1966.

Weinstock, Herbert. *What Music Is.* (Dolphin Books.) Garden City, N.Y.: Doubleday & Company.

Reference Books

Apel, Willi. *Harvard Dictionary of Music.* Cambridge, Mass.: Harvard University Press, 1954.

Baines, Anthony, Ed. *Musical Instruments Through the Ages.* Baltimore, Md.: Penguin Books, Inc., 1966.

Bauer, Marion, and Peyser, Ethel. *How Music Grew.* New York: G. P. Putnam's Sons, 1939.

———. *Music Through the Ages.* Ed. by E. E. Rogers. New York: G. P. Putnam's Sons, 1967.

Blom, Eric. *Everyman's Dictionary of Music.* Ed. by Westrup. New York: E. P. Dutton & Co., 1962.

Donington, Robert. *The Instruments of Music.* (University Paperbacks.) New York: Barnes & Noble, 1962.

Einstein, Alfred. *A Short History of Music.* New York: Alfred A. Knopf, Inc., 1947.

Ewen, David. *The Complete Book of 20th Century Music.* 2nd ed. Englewood Cliffs, N.J.: Prentice-Hall, Inc., 1959.

Mellers, Wilfrid. *Music in a New Found Land.* New York: Alfred A. Knopf, Inc., 1965.

Sachs, Curt. *A History of Musical Instruments.* New York: W. W. Norton & Company, 1940.

Schuller, Gunther. *Early Jazz.* (Basic History of Jazz Series, vol. 1.) New York: Oxford University Press, 1968.

Williams, Martin. *Jazz Masters of New Orleans.* New York: The Macmillan Company, 1967.

Wills, Vera G., and Manners, Ande. *A Parent's Guide to Music Lessons.* New York: Harper & Row, 1967.

A Sampling of Flute Recordings

The following list of recordings is a sampling of the finest of the wide range of flute music available on records. You will find some selections from the basic repertoire, as well as less familiar compositions. Both types of music are rewarding for the attentive listener. The records listed are single LP's, unless otherwise noted. Multi-record sets have been included if they feature performances of special merit or historical importance, or if they contain desirable performances that are unavailable on a single LP. The listings are drawn from the Schwann Catalog, the standard guide to Long Playing records, which is issued monthly.

Many schools have facilities for listening to records and a growing number of libraries have records available for loan. If you hear a performance that you'd like to own, investigate whether it is available on an inexpensive recording. Some of the leading record companies have budget labels that feature excellent performances and good sound at low prices. Whenever possible these inexpensive labels have been included in this discography.

Classical

Albinoni, Tommaso (1674–1745)

Concerto in G for Flute and Strings; Linde, Sacher, Zurich Collegium Musicum. Deutsche Grammophon Gesellschaft (DGG) Archive ARC-198466.

Bach, Carl Philipp Emanuel (1714–88)

Concerti for Flute and Orchestra; Linde, with Lucerne Festival Strings under Paumgartner. Deutsche Grammophon Gesellschaft (DGG) Archive ARC-198435.

Concerto in D Minor for Flute and Strings; Linde, Lucerne Festival Strings under Paumgartner. Deutsche Grammophon Gesellschaft (DGG) Archive ARC-198435. (See entry above).

Duo in G for Flute and Violin; Rampal, Baron. Dover 7264.

Sonata in A Minor for Flute Unaccompanied; Monteux. Music Guild S-147.

Sonatas (11) for Flute and Harpsichord; Rampal, Veyron-Lacroix. Nonesuch 71034.

Bach, Johann Christian (1735–82)

Quartet in F (Flute), opus 8, No. 4; Rampal, Gendre, Lepauw, Bex. Oiseau-Lyre 60018.

Sinfonia Concertante in C for Flute, Oboe, Violin, and Cello; Galway, Wickens, Armon, N. Jones, L. Jones. Nonesuch 71165.

Bach, Johann Sebastian (1685–1750)

Brandenburg Concerto No. 5 in D, S.1050; Loussier, Royal Philharmonic, Loussier Trio. London 21044.

Concerto in A Minor for Flute, Violin and Harpsichord;

Brüggen, M. Leonhardt, G. Leonhardt, Uittenbosch, Leonhardt Consort. Telefunken S-9552.

Sonata in A Minor for Flute Unaccompanied; Larrieu. Mercury SR-2-9125 (2-record set).

Sonatas (7) for Flute and Harpsichord; Larrieu, Puyana. Mercury SR-2-9125. (See entry above.)

Suite No. 2 in B Minor for Flute and Strings; C. Monteux, with London Symphony under P. Monteux. London 6400.

BEETHOVEN, LUDWIG VAN (1770–1827)

Duet in G for Two Flutes; Baker, Rampal. Orpheum 9442.

Flute Chamber Music (Complete); Rampal, Larde, Hongne, Veyron-Lacroix. Vox SVBX-577 (3-record set).

Serenade in D for Flute, Violin and Piano, opus 41; Rampal et al. Vox. (See entry above.)

Serenade in D for Flute, Violin and Viola, opus 25; Rampal, Jarry, Collott. Decca 710116.

Sonata in B-flat for Flute and Piano, opus 107; Rampal et al. Vox. (See Beethoven: *Flute Chamber Music, Complete.*)

Symphony No. 6 in F ("The Pastoral"), opus 68; Chicago Symphony under Reiner. RCA Victor LSC-2614.

Variations for Flute and Piano, opus 107; Rampal et al. Vox. (See Beethoven: *Flute Chamber Music, Complete.*)

Varied Themes (6) for Flute and Piano, opus 105; Rampal et al. Vox. (See above entry.)

BOCCHERINI, LUIGI (1743–1805)

Quintet in E-flat for Flute; Adeney, Hass, with London Baroque Ensemble. Westminster 9012.

BOISMORTIER, JOSEPH BODIN DE (1691–1755)

Concerti (6) for Five Flutes, opus 15; Rampal, Baron,

Bennett, Schaefer, Robison, Soyer, Veyron-Lacroix. Connoisseur Society S-362.

DEBUSSY, CLAUDE (1862–1918)

Prélude à l'Après-midi d'un Faune; Philadelphia Orchestra under Ormandy. Columbia MS-6883.

Sonata No. 2 for Flute, Viola, and Harp; Baker, Fuchs, Newell. Decca 9777.

Syrinx, for Flute Unaccompanied; Baker. Decca 9777 (see above entry).

DITTERSDORF, KARL DITTERS VON (1739–99)

Concerto in E Minor for Flute and Orchestra; Redel, with Munich Pro Arte Chamber Orchestra. Westminster 17060.

DVOŘÁK, ANTONIN (1841–1904)

Slavonic Rhapsodies (3), opus 45; Somogyi, with Vienna State Opera Orchestra. Music Guild S-833.

FASCH, JOHANN FRIEDRICH (1688–1758)

Sonata for Flute, Two Recorders, and Continuo; Linde, Scheck, Hampe, Koch, Muller. Deutsche Grammophon Gesellschaft (DGG) Archive ARC-198175.

FLAGELLO, NICHOLAS (1928–)

Concerto Antoniano for Flute and Orchestra (1953), *Burlesca for Flute and Guitar* (1961); Sigurdson, Flagello, with Orchestra Sinfonia Roma. Serenus 12004.

FREDERICK II, THE GREAT (1712–86)

Concerto No. 3 for Flute; Frankenland State Symphony. Lyrichord 51.

Sonatas (25); Rampal, Veyron-Lacroix. Everest 3180.

FUKUSHIMA, KAZUO (1930–)

Hi-kyo for Flute, Strings, and Percussion; Gazzelloni, Maderna, with Rome Symphony soloists. RCA Victor VICS-1313.

GRIEG, EDVARD (1843–1907)
Peer Gynt Suites, Nos. 1 & 2, opus 46, 55; Moscow Radio Symphony under Rozhdestvensky. Melodiya/Angel S-40048.

HANDEL, GEORGE FRIDERIC (1685–1759)
Sonatas for Flute (7), Nos. 1, 2, 4, 5, 7, 9, 11; Wummer, Valenti. Westminster 49084 (4-record set).

HAYDN, FRANZ JOSEPH (1732–1809)
Concerto for Flute; Linde, Collegium Aureum. RCA Victor VICS-1324.

HOTTETERRE, JACQUES (?–1760)
Pièces pour la Flûte; Harnoncourt, Vienna Concentus Musicus. Vanguard C-10029.

JOLIVET, ANDRÉ (1905–)
Concerto for Flute and Strings (1949); Rampal, with Lamoureux Orchestra under Jolivet. Music Guild S-141.

KRAUS, JOSEPH MARTIN (1756–92)
Duo in D for Flute and Viola; Monteux, Trampler. Music Guild S-147.

LOEILLET, JACQUES (1685–1746)
Concerto in D for Flute and Strings; Monteux, with St. Martin's Academy under Marriner. Oiseau-Lyre S-279.

MARTINŮ, BOHUSLAV (1890–1959)
Sonata No. 1 for Flute and Piano (1945); Baker, Makas. Westminster 17121.

MENDELSSOHN, FELIX (1809–47)
Midsummer Night's Dream, Incidental Music; Cleveland Orchestra under Szell. Columbia MS-7002.

MOZART, WOLFGANG AMADEUS (1756–91)
Andante in C for Flute and Orchestra K.315; Baker, with Solisti di Zagreb under Jaigro. Vanguard 71153.
Concerto No. 1 in G for Flute K.313; Kincaid, with Phila-

delphia Orchestra under Ormandy. Columbia MS-6451.

Concerto No. 2 in D for Flute K.314; Nicolet, with Lucerne Festival Strings under Paumgartner. DGG 136547.

Concerto in C for Flute and Harp K.299; Baron, Grandjany, with Musica Aeterna under Waldman. Decca 710075.

The Magic Flute K.620; Lemnitz, Berger, Rosswänge, Hüsch, Strienz, with Berlin Philharmonic under Beecham. Turnabout 4111/3 (3-record set).

QUANTZ, JOHANN JOACHIM (1697–1773)

Concerti for Flute; Barwahser, with Amsterdam Chamber Orchestra. Telefunken S-9429.

Concerto in G for Flute and Strings; Barwahser, with Vienna Symphony under Paumgartner. Philips 900049.

Concerto No. 17 in D for Flute; Monteux, with St. Martin's Academy under Marriner. Oiseau-Lyre S-279.

Duets (6) for Two Flutes, opus 2; Baker, Rampal. Orpheum 9419.

Sonatas for Flute, opus 1; Rampal. Everest 3180.

Trio Sonata in C for Flute, Recorder, and Continuo; Larrieu Instrumental Ensemble. Odyssey 32160086.

Trio Sonata in D for Flute, Violin, and Continuo; London Ensemble. Nonesuch 71004.

RIETI, VITTORIO (1898–)

Partita for Flute, Oboe, String Quartet, and Harpsichord; Marlowe, Baron, Chamber Orchestra. Decca 710135.

SCHOENBERG, ARNOLD (1874–1951)

Quintet for Flute, Oboe, Clarinet, Horn, and Bassoon, opus 26; Danzi Quintet. Philips WS 9068.

SCHUBERT, FRANZ (1797–1828)

Introduction and Variations for Flute and Piano, opus 160; Rampal. Everest 3165.

TCHAIKOVSKY, PETER ILYITCH (1840–1893)
Suites (4), opus 43, 53, 55, 61; Dorati, with New Philharmonia Orchestra. Mercury SR-3-9018 (3-record set).

TELEMANN, GEORG PHILIPP (1681–1767)
Concerti for Flute and Orchestra; Rampal, Veyron-Lacroix. Nonesuch 71038.
Concerto in B-flat for Two Flutes, Two Oboes, and Strings; Esterhazy Orchestra under Blum. Bach Guild 70679.

VIVALDI, ANTONIO (1678–1741)
Concerti for Flute and Orchestra; Wummer, with New York Philharmonic Orchestra under Bernstein. Columbia MS-6131.
Concerti for Flute, Violin, Bassoon, and Cembalo; Tassinari, Giangrandi, Semprini, Eggmann. Dover 5216.
Concerto for Flute, Oboe, and Bassoon; Philadelphia Woodwind Quintet. Columbia CMS-6799.

WAGNER, RICHARD (1813–83)
The Flying Dutchman: Overture; Vienna Philharmonic under Georg Solti. London 6245.

WILDER, ALEC (1907–)
Sonata for Flute, Piccolo, and Alto Flute; Hammond. Golden Crest 7005.

WUORINÉN, ALEC (1938–)
Chamber Concerto for Flute and Ten Players; Sollberger, with Group for Contemporary Music, Columbia University. Composers Recordings S-230.

Jazz (listed by performers)

COLLETTE, WILLIAM MARCEL (Buddy)
Men of Many Parts. Contemporary 3522.
Nice Day. Contemporary 3531.

HORN, PAUL

In India with Shankar. World Pacific 21445.

Jazz Suite. RCA Victor LSP-3414.

LATEEF, YUSEF (WILLIAM EVANS)

A-flat, G-flat, and C. Impulse S-9117.

Golden Flute. Impulse S-9125.

Lateef at Cranbrook. Cadet 634.

Prayer to the East. Savoy 12117.

Sounds. Prestige S-7398.

MANN, JAY SOLOMON (Herbie)

At the Village Gate. Atlantic S-1380.

Live at Newport. Atlantic S-1413.

New Mann at Newport. Atlantic S-1471.

Sound. Verve 68527.

SHANK, CLIFFORD EVERETT (Bud)

Folk in Flute. World Pacific 21819.

WESS, FRANK

North, East, South, and Wess. Savoy 12072.

Opus the Blues. Savoy 12142.

Trombones and Flute. Savoy 12086.

Virtuoso Performance Recordings

Art of the Flute; Rampal. Everest 3194 (7-record set).

Flute; Hammond. Golden Crest 7005.

Flutists' Showcase. Golden Crest 4020.

Recorder Music; Brüggen. Decca 710049. . . . Brüggen, Harnoncourt, Leonhardt. Telefunken S-9482. . . . Krainis Consort. Kapp 3385/6 (2-record set) . . . . Taylor Recorder Consort. Bach Guild 5057.

Index